Living in
Harry's World

by

Denis Deasy

**Grosvenor House
Publishing Limited**

The right of Denis Deasy to be identified as the author of this
work has been asserted in accordance with Section 78
of the Copyright, Designs and Patents Act 1988

The book cover picture is copyright to Denis Deasy

This book is published by
Grosvenor House Publishing Ltd
28-30 High Street, Guildford, Surrey, GU1 3EL.
www.grosvenorhousepublishing.co.uk

A CIP record for this book
is available from the British Library

ISBN 978-1-78148-954-3

Dedication

This book is dedicated to my wife, Joanmarie, and my sons, Denis and James. It's pointless to express in words how much I love you.

Acknowledgement

This book would not have been possible without the help of Sally Cline, Cliff McNish, Sean Poole and Lisa Jewell. Thank you for taking the time to read my book (several times) and for your guidance and constant encouragement. It is greatly appreciated.

Fat Controller

'Daddy, I want to hug the Fat Controller.'

'Leave him be, he has enough children pestering him right now.'

My son Harry and I are on a steam engine train disguised as *Thomas the Tank Engine*. A grumpy looking middle-aged man is dressed as the Fat Controller, the only human character from the famous *Thomas* books.

'Did you know that in America, the Fat Controller is called Sir Topham Hat?' I ask.

'Why?'

'American people think it's rude to call people fat.'

'Why?'

'It doesn't matter …'

Harry looks confused as another conversation between father and son peters out.

This train is more crowded than my usual five-thirty-one from Victoria. Our carriage is full of harassed mothers attempting to calm down their children after a visit from the Fat Controller, whose popularity with the kids is a mystery to me. He says nothing and seems to have landed the job solely on the basis that he's vastly overweight.

'Diarrhoea,' shouts Harry.

The noise in the carriage dramatically drops, as everyone stares at him.

'Harry, please keep your voice down,' I say, trying to remain calm.

'But I like diarrhoea.'

I hear sniggers from some of the children and murmurs of disapproval from a few of the mothers.

'Daddy, you had diarrhoea on Thursday the twenty-second of November two thousand and twelve. Did you enjoy it?'

'Can we talk about this later?'

Harry looks disappointed, but doesn't pursue the subject.

Harry's twelfth birthday is tomorrow. He was diagnosed with autism two days before his fourth birthday.

He also suffers from Attention Deficient Hyperactivity Disorder, for which he has to take daily Ritalin tablets.

'Daddy, why is Mummy thin and you're fat?' my son enquires as we depart the train.

'I'm not fat,' I respond, knowing that Harry's comments are more accurate than mine. He's completely unaware how hurtful his remarks can sometimes be. I know that I have a weight problem, but I simply haven't got the energy or the inclination to do anything about it.

'I heard Mummy's friend Jane say that you've got fat.'

'When did you hear this?'

'Last Tuesday in Mummy's house at twelve minutes past seven in the evening.'

The media always seem to portray autistic children as having a special talent. From my experience this assumption is a myth, nevertheless, my son has a photographic memory for dates.

'Do you think that I look like the Fat Controller?'

'Yes.'

Just as I'm thinking that it's time to renew my gym membership, Harry speaks again.

'I wish Mummy had a beard.'

'Harry, only men have beards.'

'But Mrs Willis has a moustache.'

Mrs Willis is one of Harry's teachers.

'No she doesn't, she has a little hair on her face, that's all.'

'I told her that I liked her moustache.'

'Was she annoyed?' I ask nervously.

'No. She walked out of the room.'

'In your next lesson why don't you tell her that she looks pretty?'

'But she's ugly.'

'Just pretend that she's pretty.'

'She's not pretty.'

'OK, just be good in her lesson and don't talk about her appearance.'

We get into our car and drive out of the train station car park.

'Where do you want to eat tonight?'

'McDonalds.'

'No, we went there last weekend; shall we go to Mario's?'

Harry doesn't respond.

Some parents of autistic children always avoid the normal family outings, like eating in restaurants or going on holiday, because it will inevitably produce stressful and embarrassing moments. I believe that Harry should experience everything that a normal child of his age does and for the past few years Harry and

I have always gone abroad for our holiday. Our flight to Italy last summer was particularly stressful, as Harry constantly kicked the seat in front of him. Inevitably the passenger complained and who could blame him? Fortunately we were upgraded to business class.

Our Italian trip wasn't a success as Harry kept complaining that the Italians were too noisy and wouldn't speak English. Although Harry couldn't watch his favourite television programmes, he did sit through endless incomprehensible Italian cartoons. Harry's birthday is tomorrow and one of his presents is a portable DVD player so at least he'll be able to watch his beloved *Thomas The Tank Engine* anywhere in the world. This may sound morbid but I'm determined to ensure that Harry will go on interesting holidays now, because when I get older I may be unable to take him.

As I have a lot of holiday time owing to me, I've taken ten days off work. I'm looking forward to spending some time with my son.

Mario's is crowded but we manage to get a table. I order lasagne for me and pizza with French fries for Harry.

'Are you excited about the concert?'

Harry nonchalantly shrugs his shoulders.

There's a concert for musical protégés at the Royal Festival Hall on Saturday week. Playing at the concert will be a twenty-five-piece orchestra, backed by a thirty-strong choir. Harry and his five class mates will be singing their own song. They will be the only special needs performers.

I felt extremely proud when the headmistress informed me of Harry's inclusion. I cannot believe that Harry will be singing on the same stage that my favourite singer, Frank Sinatra, had once graced. However, as the concert date draws nearer I'm becoming increasingly nervous.

The concert starts at seven o'clock but Harry's song won't be performed until nearly eight o'clock, although they have to remain on stage throughout. The possibility that Harry will sit still and listen to classical music for an hour seems extremely unlikely. Though friends have tried to reassure me that Harry will be fine, their worried expressions indicate the opposite.

'What did you do at school yesterday?'

'I ran up the stairs.'

'That's good. What did Mr Perry teach you?'

Harry does not reply.

'Did you do English or Maths?'

A familiar perplexed expression appears on Harry's face. My son often has difficulty engaging in the simplest of conversations. I'm envious of the way some 'normal' parents interact with their children. It saddens me that I don't have that same rapport with Harry.

Harry and I are both tall and have dark hair, which in my case is a slight exaggeration, as my hair has all but disappeared. My son is a handsome boy, who normally would have had his pick of girlfriends when he grows older.

The meal arrives and despite Harry's preference for McDonalds, he finishes it before I'm halfway through mine.

'Can I have some more fries please?' Harry asks.

I get the attention of the waitress, but before I have the chance to speak, Harry dashes over to a nearby table, snatches a handful of fries from another boy's plate and devours them.

'What are you doing?' the child's father shouts at Harry, who is still staring at the remaining fries.

'I'm sorry about that, he doesn't understand ...'

'Didn't you ever teach your son any manners?'

'My son is ...'

'Your son is a rude boy, who you obviously can't control.'

'If you would stop talking for one second, *please*.'

I now have his attention, as well as all the other diners.

'My son is autistic. He doesn't even know how to dress himself in the morning, let alone grasp why he can't help himself to someone else's meal.'

'I'm sorry, I didn't realise ...'

As incidents like this have occurred many times in the past I don't feel embarrassed, however, I'm annoyed at losing my temper so easily. How can the other child's father possibly know that Harry is autistic? He doesn't show any outward physical disabilities; in fact he looks like any other child in the restaurant.

I slip the confused waitress enough money for our meals and for an extra portion of fries for the equally perplexed boy.

'But why can't I have any more fries?' Harry questions as we leave the restaurant, clearly unable to pick up on my agitated mood. For once I don't respond.

The wonderful music of Frank Sinatra and Nat King Cole accompanies us on our car journey home, which helps to put me in a better mood. Shortly after our arrival back at the house the doorbell rings. I open the door to find my ex-wife, Laura, struggling to hold a glass dish full of pasta. I immediately take it from her.

'Thanks, I thought you might need some help for the party tomorrow,' Laura says.

'That's great, come in.'

Laura and I were divorced a year ago after twelve years of marriage. Things began to deteriorate a couple of years after Harry was born. The endless sleepless nights, combined with Harry's erratic and strange behaviour, had put an unbearable strain on our relationship.

For a long period Laura took anti-depressants, but it didn't help, as she had a nervous breakdown.

As part of the divorce settlement I was given custody of Harry, simply because Laura couldn't cope. Although her mental health has greatly improved, she still seems content with this arrangement.

Laura does take some pressure off me in looking after Harry. Her part-time job as a secretary in a local accountant's office enables her to be home by the time the school bus drops Harry off at her flat after school finishes, so that I can pick him up later. My computer programming job is less flexible, and there have been many occasions when I've had to work late, resulting in Harry sleeping overnight at his mother's.

I observe Laura as she enters the kitchen. She has model-type looks: tall and slim, with long blonde hair.

'How did you get on?' she asks.

'Stuck on a train with hundreds of screaming kids – what do you think?'

'We went riding on Thomas and Dad shouted in the restaurant,' Harry adds. Laura glances at me. 'Let me guess: Harry stole someone else's chips again?' I nod my reply.

'Why didn't you stop him?'

'I was ordering him some more chips. You know how quick he is.'

'You obviously didn't have him in the corner seat, as he wouldn't escape so easily.'

'OK, I've got the message.' My irritated mood has returned.

Laura leans closer to Harry. 'You mustn't take another person's food; is that clear?'

'I was hungry.'

'Then tell Daddy and he'll get you some more food.'

'But it took a long time.'

'Waiting is good.'

Laura outstretches both of her hands, with her palms facing Harry, which is the Makaton symbol for waiting. Makaton is a sign language used in many autistic schools.

Harry doesn't respond.

'Did you enjoy your time with Daddy?'

Harry stares blankly at nothing in particular.

Laura kneels down, to be closer to him. She points at his eyes and then her own.

'Harry, looking.'

Harry has great difficulty in making eye contact. After getting him to look directly into her eyes, Laura speaks again.

'Did you have a good time?'

Harry simply nods.

'What was the best bit of the day?'

'Thomas and the fries.'

'What else did you do?'

'I drank lemonade.' There is a short pause before Harry speaks again.

'Mummy, can I watch my DVDs now?'

'Of course you can.'

Harry walks into the living room, where he settles happily on the sofa, watching *The Lion King*. As usual he recites the dialogue word for word. When he started doing this at three years of age, I remember feeling so proud at how smart he was. We didn't realize that his slow development afterwards had anything to do with autism. Like most people, Laura and I assumed that autistic children had little or no speech. However, as Harry's appropriate language skills didn't improve, we consulted a specialist. The diagnosis changed our lives forever.

Laura hovers beside the living room door. 'I'm sorry for losing my temper, I've had a stressful day.'

'Do you think mine has been a bundle of laughs?'

For the next few minutes the only noise to be heard from the kitchen is the kettle boiling.

'Sarah rang today,' Laura remarks, breaking the strained silence.

'How's she doing?'

'Struggling. I don't know how she'll cope on her own.'

Recently Jack and Sarah have been in our thoughts. They separated a month ago. Their relationship cannot handle the constant pressure of bringing up Andrew, their severely autistic child. Most of the parents of autistic children that I know are either divorced or separated.

'They've overcome their problems before.'

Laura's worried expression indicates that she doesn't share my optimism. One of the more positive aspects of having a child of special needs is that you develop an affinity with other parents in a similar position. Laura and I know Jack and Sarah as Andrew is in Harry's class. We've shared our unique experiences with

each other on numerous occasions over a bottle or two
of wine; I've missed that camaraderie.

'I'll give Jack a ring later,' I tell Laura.

Soon after her cup of tea Laura picks up her car keys
and walks into the living room.

'Harry, I'm going now, but I'll see you tomorrow
morning.'

'What presents have you got me?'

'That's a surprise.'

'I hope it's the *Thomas And Friends – It's Great
To Be An Engine* DVD.'

'You'll have to wait and see.'

'Thomas is my friend, isn't he, Mummy?'

Laura nods. We've tried to explain to Harry in the
most simplistic way that Thomas is a fictional character,
but so far he seemingly hasn't understood this.

Laura kneels down next to Harry and gently kisses
his lips.

'I hope you have a lovely day tomorrow.'

Harry wipes his lips, as is his custom whenever
anyone kisses him and continues to watch his *Lion King*
DVD.

Laura approaches the front door but hesitates
before opening it.

'Have you forgotten anything?' I ask.

'Are you doing anything on Monday evening?'

'I don't think so.'

'Good, if I can get Maria to look after Harry, do you
fancy going out for a meal? My treat.'

Maria is a helper at Harry's school. Social Services
pay her six hours a month to baby sit Harry.

'Yeah, why not. Any reason?'

'It'll be nice to talk on our own for a change, plus
I want to make sure that you finish off your lasagne this

time. That's if they let you back into the restaurant.'
Laura smiles, before getting in the car to drive the ten-
minute journey to her flat.

I'm surprised at that invitation, given our snappy
argument earlier. I can't remember the last time that
we went out as a couple. In the last year or two of our
marriage and throughout the divorce proceedings my
relationship with Laura was unbearable. Despite our
tiffs, our time apart has helped and in the last few
months we've even joked with each other occasionally,
which hasn't happened since mobile phones looked
like bricks.

Shortly afterwards I give Harry his nightly bath. He
sits motionless in the bathtub while I wash him. As
usual he shows no interest in doing anything himself,
no matter how many times I prompt him.

The most frustrating part of the day is the night-
time. Harry can happily survive on only a couple of
hours' sleep and when he awakes he needs immediate
care and attention. Unless I lie down with him until he
falls asleep, he'll wander down to the kitchen looking
for food or playing his DVDs throughout the night.
Most of the parents of autistic children that I know
have to resort to this less-than-ideal approach. After
about half-an-hour of lying next to Harry, I turn away
from him and reach for a book on the side table. My
son immediately sits up to check that the duvet is still
covering every inch of my body, with the exception
of my head. As my arms are exposed he takes the book
away from me and tucks the duvet tight around me.
Once he's satisfied with the bedding arrangements,
he settles down again happily. Luckily it's been a cool
summer so far.

'It's your birthday tomorrow,' I mention to Harry. Tomorrow is only fifteen minutes away.

'Can we see the *Minions* film? It's on at twelve o'clock, ten minutes past two and twenty minutes past four.'

Whenever we go to the cinema, he'll always inform me that we need a maximum of seventeen minutes for the car journey, three minutes for the walk from the car to the cinema, nine minutes queuing-up time for the tickets, seven minutes for the lemonade and popcorn and a further five minutes to get to our seats.

'We won't have time, as everyone will be coming around to the house at two. Why don't I buy you a James Bond DVD instead? You liked the last one.'

'Can James Bond be in our family?'

'No, it's just the three of us. Now try to settle down.'

Harry looks confused, but is still inquisitive.

'Can Arsenal Football club come around to my house?'

'No, they're busy at the moment.'

I have this image of opening the front door to find the Arsenal manager, Arsene Wenger, standing outside; behind him are twenty-five footballers, the coaching, administration and ground staff, directors and the tea lady.

Harry cannot understand why we're not the best of friends with famous people. Then again, I'm a bit like that.

My son settles down and is quiet for a long time, enough for me to believe that he's falling asleep; I'm wrong.

'Thomas was cross when Percy crashed into him,' Harry suddenly blurts out.

'That's a shame.'

Harry has been talking about *Thomas the Tank Engine* nearly every day since he was two years old. Autistic children have great difficulty understanding emotions, but the exaggerated fixed facial expressions on the trains makes it easier for them to identify with the type of emotion shown. Consequently Harry isn't alone in his Thomas obsession. I had a lovely dream the other night where a head-on collision occurred between Thomas and Percy. No human fatalities occurred, but both of the trains died. Listening to those Thomas DVDs most days of the week for too many years has been Chinese torture. The school have advised us to wean him off Thomas to diversify his interests, but so far there haven't been too many volunteers from the school to help me manage this impossible task.

'It's time to go to sleep now,' I tell Harry.

'Sleeping is silly.'

'If you don't sleep soon you'll be very tired at your birthday party.'

'I like being tired.'

I lean over and kiss his forehead.

'Goodnight, son.'

It must be around one o'clock when I doze off.

Four hours later I awake in the same bed, but minus Harry. I dash downstairs to find him in the kitchen eating crisps and holding an open can of lemonade. Kit Kat and Starburst wrappers on the kitchen counter indicate that he's been having a feast.

'How many times have I told you about eating sweets first thing in the morning?' I shout out of frustration, before taking away all his goodies. I'm sure that raising my voice, in addition to my blood pressure, sixty seconds after waking up is not the best way to start the day.

'But my belly needs Starbursts.'

'If you want to go downstairs just ask me and we'll go down together.'

'But you weren't awake at two minutes past four.'

'Have you had any sleep?'

'Yes, I had two hours and twenty-six minutes sleep.'

'Come on, let's go back up to bed.'

Harry eagerly runs up the stairs and straight into his bedroom.

I allow him to play one of his Thomas DVDs in the faint hope that he might get tired and eventually fall asleep. I make a rare visit to my own bedroom and wearily lie on the bed. The last thing that I remember before falling asleep is hearing Harry happily singing a song about Thomas being a really useful engine.

Harry's Birthday

At ten minutes past six, I'm having breakfast with Harry. Lennon and McCartney were still writing songs together the last time I had a lie-in.

Harry has a bowl of cornflakes, without any milk. As usual he smells his cornflakes before eating any. Although nothing ever passes his lips before going through this ritual, overall, his eating habits are fairly ordinary. Simon, his school friend, has only ham sandwiches for lunch and dinner, seven days a week. He refuses to eat anything else. 'Daddy, what's Figaro's middle name?'

Figaro is our cat.

'Cats don't have middle names.'

'Peter's middle name is Christopher, Robert's is Joseph, Simon's is Alec ...'

'OK, Harry, finish off your breakfast.'

Harry has discovered the middle name of virtually everyone that he knows and recites them to me every day.

'Shall we go to see Grandma on Sunday?' I ask, attempting to distract Harry from his middle-name monologue.

'She's fired,' Harry replies. What DVD does that line come from?

Grandma is getting increasing nervous of Harry. He always gives her bear hugs that take her breath away. The last time we met up, Harry kept telling her to take a hike. I've tried to reassure my mother that he is unaware of its meaning, but she was confused and hurt by several remarks that he made that day. Perhaps we'll skip our weekend visit to her.

Although his birthday party isn't until lunchtime, I can't resist handing him one of his presents. He immediately rips open the wrapping paper but looks disappointed at its contents.

'Look, a Theo Walcott England shirt,' I proclaim in an excited manner.

'Who's he?'

'He plays for the England football team.'

Harry grimaces, then throws the shirt onto the dining-room table before rushing out to the garden to play on his trampoline.

Although this isn't an unexpected reaction, I'm still disappointed. Perhaps it's a selfish wish on my part to think that my son might take even a little interest in a present that most twelve-year-olds would love to receive. What a pity there isn't a famous footballer called Thomas.

At midday Harry is still in the garden. I watch him from the kitchen as he sits on the grass, intently studying the movement of ants.

'Harry, don't eat the bugs; we're having the cake soon,' I remind him, before the sound of the doorbell interrupts me. I open the door to find Laura holding a carrier bag full of presents.

'How's he doing? Is he excited?' Laura asks, as she enters the house.

'He was first thing this morning, but Theo Walcott changed that.'

Laura looks understandably confused.

'He didn't like the England shirt,' I explain.

Laura sighs as she puts the gifts on the dining-room table. She's not a great football fan and took it personally whenever I decided to watch Arsenal on a Saturday afternoon, rather than spend time with her. In the end the hassle wasn't worth it, so I gave up Arsenal.

'Happy birthday, Harry,' Laura enthusiastically greets her son, as she approaches him in the garden.

Harry doesn't look up at his mother, which isn't unusual. I get a similar reaction every day whenever I pick him up at Laura's flat. We cannot compete with the charismatic personalities of the ants.

Nevertheless, Laura gives him an affectionate hug and for a brief second Harry glances up at the person who's invading his privacy.

'Did you like Daddy's present?

'It's crap.'

'Daddy wants you to play more football. Wouldn't you like to do that?'

'I wanted a Thomas DVD.'

'You'll be getting all the rest of your presents soon, so don't give up hope yet.'

'Trains don't play football, do they, Mummy?'

'Not that I'm aware of.'

Laura and I have always tried to get Harry involved in a team sport but he's never been interested. Last season I took him along to watch Arsenal play a few times. Although he seemed to enjoy the games, especially when the crowds sang, he's never followed up his interest once the match is over. This apathy in participating in and watching sport is also shared by all of Harry's autistic friends.

Soon afterwards Laura and I are having a cup of tea in the kitchen.

'So where will you be holidaying this year?' Laura enquires.

'I'm not sure; maybe Disney World.'

'The flight will be a bit traumatic though, won't it?'

'Probably, but we'll manage.'

'Harry won't like the queues at Disney World. Have you forgotten what happened the last time?'

'I'm getting a letter from the doctor about Harry's autism. The customer service department at Disney World will then give me an exit pass, which means that we'll go to the front of the queue on every ride.'

The last family holiday that we had together was to Disney World. The whole trip was a disaster for many reasons. However, Harry is two years older now and I'm also hopeful that this magical exit pass will reduce the stress.

'It sounds like you've thought of everything.'

'Why are you being negative?'

'The noise and the crowds will upset him again.'

'I'm not that stupid, I know what he's like – after all I do live with him seven days a week.'

'That's unfair,' Laura retorts.

'I know and I'm sorry, but I hate it when you lecture me about Harry.'

'I didn't mean it like that. I worry about him.'

'And I don't?'

As I'm walking towards the kitchen sink, I notice that Harry is beginning to take his clothes off in the garden.

'Look I better get out there. Can we resume this argument later?'

'I don't want to argue with you on Harry's birthday, or any other day come to that.'

'Good, so let's enjoy the rest of the day then, shall we?'

For some reason my mind goes back to that dreadful day eight years ago when we found out about Harry's autism.

Harry was a disruptive child in his nursery class and on many occasions the school contacted me or Laura to take him home early due to one incident or another.

I was at the checkout in Sainsbury's one evening when a lady approached me to let me know that she had to change nurseries for her son Adrian, because Harry kept beating him up. I knew that Adrian had left, but had no idea why. Understandably she was extremely angry towards me. I apologised several times, but that didn't stop the tirade.

I felt such great sympathy for her and Adrian, and utter despair for Harry's never ending problems.

I cried all the way home.

Harry's behaviour was becoming increasingly unpredictable. He hardly slept, would throw his dinner on the floor if it wasn't to his taste and never showed any affection for me and Laura. To this day we have to instruct him to give us a hug.

Harry had a reasonable vocabulary from an early age, which deceived us from going down the autistic road.

We spent several months seeing a child physiologist, who taught us numerous behavioural management techniques; all to no avail.

One afternoon we visited a relative and was shocked to see how more advanced our niece, Melissa, was compared to Harry, even though she was nine months younger than him.

It finally dawned on us that Harry's problems may be deeper than we thought.

On a referral from our doctor we met up with three autistic specialists in Guys hospital in London. Harry spent the morning going through rigorous tests and even though we knew the reason why we were there, when they ultimately told us their findings, we were stunned. 'Harry is on the autism spectrum,' is how one of the specialists told us. After those six words were spoken all I can remember is seeing all their lips moving up and down, but I didn't hear another word. Laura and I couldn't speak to each other for about an hour afterwards and seemed to walk aimlessly around London.

Our first reaction was why us? We were told that both parents have to carry the autistic gene and although they took blood samples from us there was no further investigation. Laura wanted to pursue this, but I thought that it was pointless. Harry is, and always will be autistic. Nothing will change that.

It ultimately destroyed Laura's health and then our marriage.

By the time I arrive in the garden, Harry is running around the trampoline completely naked and laughing hysterically. He loves nothing better than taking off his clothes, whether it's in the middle of summer or the coldest day of winter. After chasing him for a few minutes, I eventually manage to catch up with him and put his clothes back on, knowing that in a short while he'll try the same thing again.

If my next-door neighbour ever films some of the antics that go on in my garden, he can make a few pounds by selling the tape to one of those funny home videos TV programmes.

My younger sister, Fiona, and her daughter Isabelle arrive at midday.

Fiona has my dark features but Isabelle, with her blonde hair and blue eyes, is the image of her father. Isabelle is two weeks away from her tenth birthday.

'Why don't you go and play with Harry?' Fiona asks her, as they enter the kitchen. Isabelle doesn't look pleased at this prospect.

'He's in the garden,' I tell her. Isabelle slowly walks out to the garden. From the kitchen I closely observe her.

'Happy birthday, Harry,' Isabelle mumbles.

'Thomas is a blue engine and James is red,' Harry responds.

'If you say so.' Isabelle's bored expression indicates that she'd rather be anywhere else than in my garden with my son. Soon afterwards she's back in the house.

'Uncle David, can I log onto Harry's ipad please?'

'Yeah, you'll probably find it on his bed.'

As conversation with Harry is rarely straightforward, most children tend to ignore him. Although I recognise that children need some sort of interaction, I get increasingly frustrated when family members behave in the same way.

I walk out to the garden and sit next to Harry.

Harry has always been an insular child. At social gatherings all the other children would play together, while my son wanted to be on his own. This breaks my heart, knowing that he'll always be different from everyone else.

'Are you having a good day?'

Harry is still focused on the ants' activities.

'Harry, look at Daddy.'

He eventually looks in my direction.

'Are you enjoying yourself?'

'I love ants.'

'What's so great about them?'

'They're always busy and I like to eat them.'

'I suppose that's two good reasons. What do you want to do tomorrow?'

'Go riding on Thomas.'

'No, we did that yesterday. What about going to Brighton? You enjoyed our last visit there, didn't you?'

'We went to Brighton on Saturday June the fourteenth. My train fare cost eight pounds and the train journey took sixty-one minutes.'

'Would you like to go swimming in the sea?'

'It's too noisy.'

'What about playing some of the games in the arcade?'

'No, there are cobwebs on the ceiling. I don't like cobwebs.'

'There must be something you enjoyed in Brighton?'

'I liked going on the train.'

'I thought you might say that,' I reply, as Fiona approaches us.

'Hi, Harry,' Fiona says as she hands Harry his present, but her eyes seem to be showing more interest in our new trampoline. 'I love the trampoline, was it expensive?'

'I don't know. Laura bought it for his birthday.'

'I must ask Laura how much it cost.'

I make my way back into the kitchen to prepare the cake. A couple of minutes later Laura walks out to the garden carrying a glass of wine for Fiona.

Harry's class friend, Niall, and his mother Kerry, arrive soon after Fiona. Sometimes when I feel a bit low I have to remind myself that there's always someone worse off than me; two such people are Kerry and Niall. He's severely autistic and completely non-verbal. How does Kerry cope without being able to converse with her son at all? I don't always understand what's going on in Harry's mind, but his ability to speak makes it easier to communicate at some level with him.

Niall is slightly shorter and chubbier than Harry. His dark looks resemble his mother's.

Niall immediately runs out to the garden and by the time we get there he's sitting in a small space in between two rose bushes, playing with his one-legged Action Man.

'Is he OK there?' I ask Kerry.

'He's fine. A chair would be far too conventional.'

After chatting to Laura and Fiona in the garden, Kerry then joins me in the kitchen.

'Thanks for coming along,' I tell her.

'We're grateful for the invite. We don't get asked to parties that often, apart from a couple autistic ones, that is.'

'Yeah, I know what you mean. Let's get this party started; what'll you have, red or white?' I hold a bottle of each.

'Red please. David, do you mind if I pop upstairs to check that all the windows are shut, before Niall does his Spiderman impression?'

'Don't worry, all the upstairs windows have been locked since Harry was about two.'

I understand Kerry's relieved look only too well. Whenever I visit another person's house I always check that all the windows are closed. I'm sure people think that I'm paranoid and acting like a demented Secret Service agent, but there have been too many dangerous episodes in the past for me to take any chances.

'David, I'd better go back out there, I don't want Niall eating any of your flowers.'

'I think you'll find that there's very few left uneaten,' I respond in acknowledgement of another one of Harry's party tricks.

Kerry takes a sip of her wine. 'I usually polish off a bottle of this stuff before midday if I'm feeling tense.'

'Really?'

'No, I'm only joking, although I've been known to drink a glass or two when Niall is asleep.'

'And why not?'

'How are things between you and Laura now?'

I've only met Kerry a handful of times at various school events, but despite our casual acquaintance she can be extremely direct with me.

'We have our moments, but overall not bad. Where's Danny?'

'He left me three months ago. He'd been having an affair with someone at work for the past year. I didn't suspect a thing.'

'I'm sorry to hear that, it must be a difficult time for you.'

Kerry simply nods her response.

An embarrassing silence interrupts our conversation. Given my precarious relationship with Laura, I'm hardly the best person to be giving out advice on marital problems, especially to someone I don't know that well.

Kerry picks up her wine glass, gives me a brief smile before joining her son in the garden.

One of the new skills I've acquired since my split with Laura is learning how to bake. I've spent hours baking a chocolate fudge cake for Harry, and I cannot wait to show it off. I take the cake out of the fridge and carefully place it on the dining-room table before going back into the kitchen in search of birthday candles. Upon my return Harry is sitting at the table holding the cake.

'Harry, put that down.'

He promptly bites into the cake and uses his hand to scoop another piece into his mouth. Harry always needs constant reminding to use the kitchen utensils, but why bother with the middle man? Isabelle is standing a couple of feet away, smiling.

'Come over here and let me clean you up,' I say, trying hard not to sound too annoyed.

Harry is still licking his fingers as he walks towards me. I wash his hands and face and shortly afterwards we're all singing happy birthday in front of a dilapidated cake. As Harry blows out the candles, he smiles for the first time today.

Laura compliments me on how delicious the cake is, but declines to give me marks out of ten for presentation.

The first birthday present that he opens is an expensive-looking Ralph Lauren shirt from Fiona. Harry looks disgusted. 'That shirt is rubbish.'

'Fiona spent a long time looking for a nice shirt for you, so don't be rude to her.'

'I've got clothes already, I wanted DVDs.'

'You've got enough DVDs, now are you going to thank Fiona?'

'Thanks.' Harry's response lacks any sort of conviction as his eyes are now focused on the next present, which he knows is a DVD.

'Harry, you can open it now,' I reassure him.

Harry tears open the wrapping to reveal his beloved *Thomas And Friends – It's Great To Be An Engine* DVD. He punches the air with delight and immediately rushes upstairs to play it.

'I know what to get him next year,' Fiona mumbles with a wry smile.

I'm about to tell Harry to come downstairs, when Laura comes over to me and puts her arm on my shoulder. 'David, let him play his DVD, he can open up the rest of his presents later.'

I look over at Niall who is standing by the dining-room door, staring out into the garden. He's constantly pulling and prodding his one-legged Action man, whom I fear will soon be without another leg or arm. I approach him.

'Niall, do you want to go outside?'

He starts to hit his forehead with his fist. I kneel down next to him and gently hold his hands. To show his displeasure at my intervention, he head-butts me. It's a head-butt that the local yob a few doors down would have been proud of, and for a few seconds I see stars. When my vision returns, Niall is still staring at the garden as if nothing has happened. Kerry rushes towards me.

'Are you OK?'

'Don't worry, I'm fine. I didn't expect that.' I smile.

Kerry turns to Niall.

'No hitting, is that clear?'

Niall grits his teeth and hits his forehead again. Kerry holds both of his hands until he eventually calms down.

'You mustn't hurt David,' Kerry explains.

Niall starts to laugh, but still will not take his eyes off the garden.

'Kerry, don't worry, it's not a problem. I presume he wants to go outside?'

'Yes, but he has to apologise first. Niall go over and be nice to David,' Kerry reiterates, pointing in my direction.

Niall eventually makes his way over to me and gently strokes my arm. Even though Niall is mentally handicapped, Kerry still makes sure that he apologises for what she deems inappropriate behaviour. I know some parents of normal children who should take heed.

'Good boy. Do you want to go out to the garden?' Kerry asks.

Niall takes Kerry's hand and directs it onto the door handle. We all watch as he escapes the house and settles amongst the rose bushes again.

'Now you know why we don't get invited to other parties,' Kerry mutters, in a resigned tone.

'Would it help his speech if he spent more time around normal children?' Fiona questions.

As Niall attends an autistic school he mostly interacts with autistic children. However, his lack of speech, due to his severe autism, is far too complex to be solved by hanging around non-autistic children.

'It's not quite as simple as that,' Kerry snaps, without going into any more detail. She then strolls back into the garden and sits alongside Niall, helping him play games with his Action Man, but Niall isn't interested in any role playing, his sole aim is to remove an arm, leg or head.

Laura comes over to me and examines my forehead. 'You're going to have a big bruise there in the morning.'

'If anyone asks, I got this by taking on a couple of teenage yobs,' I explain, pointing to the read mark on my forehead.

'Instead of saying that a twelve-year-old boy did it?'

A short time later Fiona and Isabelle come over.

'David, we've got to leave now,' Fiona says, 'I've got Jack's dinner to prepare.'

Jack is Fiona's husband.

'Lovely to see you, Fiona, and thanks again for your present.'

'We had a nice time, didn't we, Isabelle?'

Isabelle nods her reply, without conviction.

'Harry come downstairs and say goodbye to Fiona and Isabelle,' I shout in the direction of his bedroom.

Within seconds Harry comes rushing down the stairs and literally jumps into Fiona's arms, knocking her back a few steps.

'Harry, take it easy, don't hurt Fiona.'

'But I wanted to hug her.'

'Hug gently,' I remind him, although Harry doesn't seem to be listening.

'Why is your bum so big?' Harry asks my sister.

Fiona is speechless, while Isabelle starts to giggle.

'Harry, that's rude. Now you apologise to Fiona.'

'But her bum is much bigger than Mummy's and Niall's mum.'

'Fiona's bum is not big, now you say sorry to her,' I tell my son, although I feel awkward talking about my sister's posterior.

Harry does not respond, so Laura kneels down next to him.

'Daddy's right, you mustn't be rude to people.'

'But I don't like big bums, they look stupid.'

'Don't worry, Laura, I'd better be getting back,' Fiona says, as she quickly opens the front door.

Laura and I hug Fiona before she gets into her car. I can see from her expression that her feelings are hurt and I feel sorry for her. As they drive off I notice that Isabelle is still smiling.

After Fiona leaves, Laura and I walk out to the garden.

'How's Niall doing?' Laura asks Kerry.

'He's fine now. Sometimes I can't figure out what triggers these outbursts, it's very worrying,' Kerry answers. The redness in her eyes indicates that she's been crying.

'I hope you didn't mind Fiona's comment about Niall's speech problems?' I remark.

'Of course not. Before I had Niall, the only knowledge I had of autism was watching the film *Rain Man*. Even parents of autistic children struggle to fully understand the complexities of autism, so what chance is there for the average person in the street?'

'She does have an autistic nephew, though.'

'Observing autism from a distance is very different from living with it.'

A moment of silence ensues before Kerry speaks again.

'I'm sorry for sounding so depressed on Harry's birthday.'

'Please don't worry, we understand,' Laura reassures her.

'What are your plans for Niall tomorrow?' I enquire.

'He's going to Adventurers.' Adventurers is a play scheme for children with special needs.

'Harry and I are off to Brighton for the day. Would Niall like to join us?' I ask.

Laura raises her eyebrows in surprise.

'That's very sweet of you, but as you saw today he's a handful. He'll probably kick and spit at you if he doesn't get his way.'

'Harry's class friend Simon has a similar personality. He's stayed overnight here a few times and the house is still standing.' I did lie about Simon, but I want to re-assure her.

Kerry takes a sip of wine. 'He does love going to the beach.'

'That's settled then, what time do you want me to pick him up?'

'Are you sure you want to do this?'

'Of course. It'll be a fun day out for all of us.'

'I'm starting work at nine. Is eight o'clock too early?'

'No problem. It's probably best if we exchange mobile numbers, but don't worry, I'll take good care of him.'

We manage to drag Harry away from his Thomas viewing to open the rest of his presents. He seems to enjoy most of them, particularly the portable DVD player. He's less than impressed with Grandma's present, which is a pair of Levis.

'Grandma has lost the plot,' Harry announces, before throwing the jeans into the rubbish bin.

'Don't worry, I'll get them back,' Laura tells me.

Throughout the present opening, his Thomas DVD never leaves his side, and immediately after opening his last present he picks it up and holds it an inch away from Niall's face.

'Niall, do you want to watch *It's Great to Be an Engine*?'

I gently pull Harry's hand back to prevent his DVD poking Niall's eye out. Although Niall isn't looking at Harry, I notice that he's smiling.

Kerry takes Niall's hand. 'Let's go to Harry's room and watch Thomas.' They both follow Harry upstairs.

Laura walks over and sits next to me.

'Do you know what you're letting yourself in for?'

'Don't you think I can take care of Niall?'

'I'm just saying that it'll be difficult to look after both Harry and Niall for the whole day.'

'Don't worry, I can handle both of them.' My outwardly confident manner probably doesn't fool Laura; I'm sure she can detect that I'm nervous. I'm already having second thoughts. A day out with Harry is usually a stressful experience, so why did I volunteer to increase my blood pressure to dangerous levels? Perhaps I felt sorry for Kerry? She seems to be having a hard time with Niall, so what chance have I got? It was an impulsive decision and perhaps a wrong one?

'Do you remember the last time we went to Brighton and Harry pulled down his swimming trucks in front of everyone and peed into the sea?' I reminisce, attempting to lighten my mood. 'He was nine years old at the time, so people did stare at us.'

'How could I forget?' Laura replies. 'There were only about a hundred thousand people on the beach to witness that one.'

After chatting for another ten minutes, Laura picks up her belongings and says goodbye to Harry, Niall and Kerry.

'Thanks for your help today,' I tell Laura.

Laura smiles. 'Take good care of the boys, I'll ring you tomorrow.'

'They'll be fine, I think Harry will enjoy having Niall with us.'

Laura nods, but looks unconvinced as she drives off. At least the day didn't end in an argument.

It isn't long afterwards when Kerry and Niall also leave.

A couple of minutes after midnight I'm lying in Harry's bed, still awake.

'My birthday's finished now. Can I have another one next week please?'

'No, it's only once a year.'

'That's not fair.' To emphasise his point Harry breaks wind for the umpteenth time in the past hour or so.

'Harry, please stop farting.'

'It keeps doing it,' Harry responds, pointing to his bottom. Social graces are not Harry's strongest point. If breaking wind ever becomes an Olympic event he'll be challenging Steve Redgrave's gold medal total.

Whenever Harry wants to do a number two, he takes all of his clothes off, irrespective of where we might be. A couple of months ago he did this in a restaurant toilet and then decided to wash his hands before putting his clothes back on. Needless to say we got some strange looks from the fellow diners.

'OK, let's go to sleep, it's an early start tomorrow.'

Shortly afterwards I doze off, but a couple of hours later my night's sleep is interrupted by the sound of running water. I dash to the bathroom, to find Harry sitting in a full bathtub.

Although empty shampoo bottles are lying on the floor, his hair is completely dry, as he has flushed all the shampoo down the toilet. I also notice that the sink is covered in toothpaste and there seems to be a shortage of soap, air-fresheners, toothbrushes and toilet rolls. After a quick glance out of the bathroom window I discover that the missing items are now decorating our garden.

This happens a couple of times a week and has been going on for the last eighteen months or so. After a severe tummy bug last winter, I was reduced to stumbling around the garden at two o'clock in the morning searching for the last toilet roll.

Harry must be developing strong arm muscles because lately my next-door neighbour has been handing me bags full of toiletries that have been deposited in his garden.

I clean Harry up, tidy the bathroom and return to his bedroom. Three hours later I awake to hear the sentence 'Bond, my name is James Bond' repeated over and over again by Pierce Brosnan. For a few sleepy seconds I'm convinced that Pierce is actually in our bedroom, but when I open my eyes I can see Harry sitting on the edge of his bed rewinding his favourite part of the James Bond DVD. Harry prefers Pierce Brosnan over Daniel Craig, as Brosnan narrated some Thomas The Tank Engine DVDs.

I soon realise that he's in no mood to go back to sleep so we both make our way downstairs, where I listen to Harry repeating that famous line countless times whilst having breakfast.

My lack of sleep over the past forty-eight hours has left me exhausted, but I hope that the combination of a long day out and the sea air will help Harry sleep better tonight.

Brighton

Kerry opens her front door.

Harry immediately runs ahead of me, and dashes upstairs.

'Why don't you come down here and say hello to Kerry?' I shout from the bottom of the stairs.

'I saw her already, now I need to play with all the Thomas stuff,' Harry replies, before disappearing into Niall's bedroom.

'That's OK, all of Niall's school friends do exactly the same. Do you fancy a cup of coffee?' Kerry asks.

'I'd love one, if you've got the time.'

'I don't have to leave for another twenty minutes.' I follow Kerry into her kitchen.

'What's your job?' I ask.

'I teach English at the local school. I only work part-time, as I need to pick up Niall from school every day.'

'Teaching must be stressful though?'

'All jobs are a pain in the arse, aren't they?'

'Yeah, I know mine is.'

'The behaviour of some of the kids frustrates me, especially when I compare their capabilities to Niall, but I know that's unfair.'

'Is Niall aware that he's going to Brighton with us?' I ask.

'I've told him a couple of times, but I'm not sure he understood.'

I nod as if I know precisely what she goes through on a daily basis, but of course I don't.

Kerry hands me a coffee.

'How much time does Danny spend with Niall?'

'None, at the moment. He's in love with some tart half his age, so why would he want to spend any time with his son?'

'Do you get any respite?' I ask, to distract Kerry elaborating further on Danny's tart.

'Social Services provide a carer one evening a month. I usually go to the pub or the cinema with a couple of friends. Whenever I ask for any more time they always tell me there's no funding, so I've given up asking.'

Niall walks into the kitchen carrying a toy horse's head, minus the body. Kerry kneels down next to him.

'Niall, say hello to David.'

Niall briefly glances at his mother, but then quickly looks away to stare at nothing in particular.

'You're going for a ride in the car with David and Harry.' Kerry holds up a PECS card in front of Niall, which displays a picture of a car.

PECS stands for Picture Exchange Communication System. It consists of a series of picture cards that show anything from a glass of orange juice to a boy going to the toilet. This especially helps the non-verbal children who can communicate their needs through the use of these cards.

'They're taking you to the beach. You like swimming in the sea, don't you?'

Niall runs into the living room without responding.

'David, can you take these cards with you? They're helpful, although he only uses the food-related ones.'

'OK.'

Kerry hands me a book full of laminated PECS cards. I'm familiar with these as they use them in Harry's school for the more severely autistic children.

'David, please hold onto him tightly near traffic. He has a tendency to run out onto the road, especially if he sees a sweet shop on the other side. You should be OK though, as he hasn't done this in a while.'

'Don't worry, I'll be careful, Harry used to do that all the time.'

'I'm sorry, I should've told you this yesterday, but I forgot. I won't mind if you decide not to take him.'

'Don't be silly, I'm looking forward to spending the day with him.'

This is a lie. I wouldn't have volunteered to look after Niall if I had known about his suicidal tendencies. But I can't back out now.

A few minutes later Harry rushes down the stairs and immediately opens the front door.

'Harry, please shut the door, we're not ready yet.'

'But we're going to be late.'

'I hope you haven't been stealing again?'

This is another one of Harry's favourite pastimes, although thankfully this hasn't extended to shops; yet.

'Of course not,' Harry says.

'Can you come here for a second?'

Harry warily walks towards me. I'm so used to giving him a body search that I'm thinking of giving private lessons to the security staff at Heathrow airport. Inevitably I find a Thomas DVD, minus its cover, stuffed inside his underpants. At least he's getting more cunning in his hiding places.

'Harry how many times must I tell you that stealing is wrong?'

'But I haven't got the *Thomas – Brave Little Engines* DVD.'

'I don't care, you mustn't take anything that doesn't belong to you.'

'How come Niall has got it and I don't?'

'He can borrow it if he likes,' Kerry whispers in my ear.

'Thanks, but no. All he had to do was ask.'

I decide not to pursue the conversation with Harry as it'll probably go on for months, so I take the DVD from him and hand it back to Kerry, who quickly hides it in a kitchen drawer. Harry walks slowly into the hallway, where he turns around to glance sadly at the drawer.

'Sorry about that, it's worrying how far he'll go to get his Thomas fix.'

'I thought that you handled it well. Danny would've probably said that it was no big deal. Anyway, I better get Niall ready.'

Kerry finds Niall staring out of the living room window onto the street. She tucks his shirt into his trousers and ties his shoelaces. She then embraces him, but Niall doesn't respond, keeping his arms firmly by his side.

'Niall, have a lovely day and don't cause David any problems.'

'He'll be fine,' I say, ' I'll give you a ring later.'

With Niall and Harry in the back of my car, I pull out of the driveway, en route to Brighton. Kerry looks concerned, but given Niall's unpredictable behaviour this is understandable.

As we're driving through our local high street, Niall starts crying and banging his head against his knee.

'Niall, what's the matter?' I ask, looking in my rear-view mirror. He reacts to my question by repeatedly kicking the back of my seat.

'He wants to go to McDonalds,' Harry mumbles.

'But it's not even nine o'clock,' I reply, forgetting that the concept of time means nothing to Niall.

'McDonalds don't have burgers and fries before eleven o'clock. The people who make them must love their sleep.' Harry says.

I drive on looking for a parking space and just as I turn around again to check on Niall, he throws one of his shoes at me. His aim is perfect as the heel hits me in the middle of my forehead. I immediately put my foot on the brake and am fortunate to avoid an accident as there are no other cars anywhere near us. I suspect that the head-butting bruise will soon be accompanied by the shoe bruise.

'No, Niall don't hurt my daddy,' Harry shouts, as I eventually find a parking space down a side road.

'Harry, that's OK, Niall doesn't understand,' I say, impressed by Harry's appropriate response.

I examine the huge red mark on my forehead. My lack of hair in this area has left me exposed for this type of attack.

'Can I throw my shoes at you when I'm angry?' Harry enquires.

'No, definitely not.'

I remember seeing a McDonalds PECS card so I search through the folder that Kerry has given me and find exactly what I need. The card shows the McDonalds symbol with a huge red cross slashed across it.

'Look, Niall, no McDonalds,' I firmly announce whilst holding the card in front of him. Niall shows his displeasure by gritting his teeth and hitting his forehead with his fist.

'No hitting,' I tell him. He eventually calms down and then starts to laugh. It baffles me how his emotions can switch from anger to amusement in a matter of seconds.

A short time later we continue our journey. When I put on a Robbie Williams CD I notice that Niall is moving his head to the rhythm of the music, Stevie Wonder style, which makes him calmer and seemingly happier. Even Harry sings along to 'Angels', which is one of the few pop songs that he likes.

Two hours later we arrive in Brighton. Despite the heavy traffic we manage to find a parking space near the sea front.

As we are all walking towards the beach, Niall tugs at my arm. Initially I don't understand why he's doing this, but when he glances over at the sweet shop on the other side of the street I realise what he's trying to communicate.

'Niall, no sweets, we're going for lunch now.' However, despite holding his hand, he breaks free from me. In my attempt to grab him, I slip and end up on the pavement. From my lowly viewpoint I watch in despair as he runs onto the road. A speeding car heads towards Niall, who is seemingly oblivious of the danger. I get up and frantically wave at the driver, who manages to swerve, missing Niall by only a few inches. I dash onto the street to bring him back to the safety of the pavement.

The driver immediately gets out of his car, leaving it in the middle of the road and walks purposefully towards us.

'I could've killed your son, why didn't you stop him?' he barks at me.

'Sorry about that, I was holding his hand but he pulled away.'

The driver looks at Niall, who is now holding my hand and smiling.

'Your son obviously thinks it's all a game. Don't you realise I could've been seriously hurt as well?'

'Niall is severely autistic, I'm afraid he just doesn't understand road safety.'

'Then you should've taken better care of him.'

The beeping from some of the vehicles backed up behind the driver's car becomes louder by the minute, so he returns to his car and drives off. As he passes us by he gives me the middle finger for good measure.

Everything he said is correct. Niall saw the sweet shop on the other side of the road and didn't care what obstacles might be in his way. I should have been more alert.

I dread telling Kerry about the incident, but that can wait until we're back at her house. I'm sure that she'll never trust me to look after her son again.

'Shall we go to McDonalds?' I ask my companions, giving in to their fast food cravings.

Harry punches the air with delight. 'Yes, bloody farts.'

Niall has already seen the McDonalds sign in the distance and is edging me towards it. Luckily it's on our side of the road.

As I approach the counter in McDonalds I have a firm grip on Harry and Niall, who are both looking at the other diners' meals, no doubt waiting for an opportunity to pounce. I order the meal and to avoid letting go of Harry and Niall, I instruct Harry to take the twenty-pound note out of my pocket with his free hand, which he does, and hands it over to the perplexed-looking McDonalds' cashier.

'Do you mind bringing the meal to our table please?' I ask the girl. She looks briefly at both Harry and Niall, before nodding in acknowledgement.

I manage to find a spot in the corner where the nearest tables to us are empty. Niall happily plays with his Action Man, who predictably is now minus his head, in addition to his missing leg. Occasionally he'll place the Action Man on the table and play with the decapitated leg instead.

'Are you excited about being in Brighton?' I ask Harry.

My son doesn't respond.

'Harry, please look at me. Are you happy to be here?'

'Why couldn't we bring Figaro? I wanted to throw her into the sea to test that she can swim.'

'Cats are scared of water.'

'I think Figaro's stupid.'

Harry is sometimes cruel to Figaro. Sitting on our cat's back, when Laura and I aren't looking, is something that brings him great joy.

'Did you enjoy the journey down here?'

'It took a long time, why didn't we travel on the train?'

'It's easier for Niall to go in the car.'

'Cars are lumps of shit.'

'Harry, you must not swear.'

'Swearing is good for me.'

'No it's not, it's very bad.'

'But you swear sometimes. On Saturday the twenty-first of February you called someone on the television a stupid, ugly bastard.'

I'm sure that Harry is referring to my comments directed at the referee during an Arsenal football match.

'I know and that was wrong, but you've been swearing too much lately and it's got to stop.'

My son looks away.

'Harry, I've never heard you practise the song for the Festival Hall concert.'

'I'm not bothered about it.'

'Do you know all the words?'

'Sometimes.'

'That's why you need to keep rehearsing. What'll happen if you forget the words when you're on the stage?'

'That'll be much better, because then I'll talk to the crowd about Thomas and Bugs Bunny; they'll love it.'

That's doubtful. Even Stephen Fry would struggle to make that subject matter interesting.

'I really want you to rehearse that song.'

'Nah, I only sing at school and this is Brighton.'

I'm delighted that Harry is playing at such a prestigious venue, but mostly I'm extremely tense, knowing that this could be a most humiliating day for all concerned.

Shortly afterwards the food is brought over. I've ordered a double portion of French fries to discourage Harry or Niall from stealing anyone else's fries. They both scoff down their meals as if they haven't eaten for days and are soon helping themselves to my burger and fries. Shortly afterwards we leave McDonalds.

'I think it's time for the beach,' I proclaim.

'I don't like the sea, it's got jellyfish in it,' Harry complains.

During a trip to Portugal three years ago Harry saw a jellyfish in the sea and has never forgotten it.

'Harry, that was in Portugal. The sea in England doesn't have any jellyfish,' I lie.

Harry doesn't look convinced.

'Can't we go to ToysRus instead?'

'No, we're going to the beach and you're going to have a lovely time.'

Trying to get Harry to do any outside activities is always a struggle. He'll happily stay in his bedroom watching his DVDs, only venturing out when it's time to eat.

While we're walking towards the beach I notice that Niall touches a number of passers-by on their arm or leg. The reaction is usually one of surprise, but only a couple of people are annoyed. I apologise to everyone, but I don't explain Niall's autism. I know some parents of autistic children, including Laura, carry a handful of autism awareness cards that are designed by the National Autistic Society. If their child misbehaves, the parent will simply hand the cards to anyone nearby. The card reads as follows – 'This young person has autism. Autism is a developmental disability that affects social and communication skills. People with autism tend to behave in an odd and unpredictable way as a result of their disability. Please help us by being understanding and showing tolerance.'

As we approach the beach Harry rushes over to an elderly man sitting on a bench reading *The Times*.

'Mister, do you have Sky?'

'I'm sorry. What did you say?'

'Do you have Sky TV?'

'I do as a matter of fact, but I'm not sure if it's any of your business.'

'I'm sorry about this,' I tell the man. 'Come on, Harry, let's go now.'

'Old men don't watch the Disney channel, so can I have yours?'

I smile at the confused man, while gently pulling Harry away. As we start to walk towards the beach Harry still turns around in case the man replies.

'You can't ask strangers for their television channels.'

'But it's so unfair. Couldn't we give him that stupid CNN channel? They're all a bunch of bald arseholes on there.'

'Harry, what did I say about swearing?'

'But it gives me energy.'

I'm about to give him another lecture on swearing when I notice that he's now focused on the sky above him.

'What are you looking at?' As if I didn't know.

'Those bastard bugs, they're out to destroy me.'

Harry has a fixation about bees and wasps, in fact any flying insect. A couple of summers ago he was stung by a bee, so to some extent I can understand his anxiety, but his obsession is carried to extremes. As soon as the hot days of summer arrive so does Harry's insect apprehension. He always makes sure that I unlock the car doors before we leave the house, so that he can dash to the safety of the car without waiting for any length of time outside.

As we're walking along the sea front Harry constantly slaps his back, shoulders and legs to deter the imaginary insect. His paranoia is such that he always thinks a bee or wasp has landed on him. This slapping routine draws some strange looks from some of the locals, who probably think that he's a demented Morris dancer.

As it is the first hot day of the summer, the beach is crowded. We make our way to the front, as I want to be nearby when Harry and Niall go swimming.

'Daddy, this beach is a bit weird, it hasn't got any sand.'

'Not all beaches have sand. Now are you going in for a swim?'

'But the bees will sting my willy.'

'The bees and wasps in Brighton don't sting.'

'But that's their job.'

'Yes, it is normally, but they only come to Brighton for a holiday.'

Harry looks at me with some suspicion, but after digesting my words of wisdom for a couple of minutes he visibly relaxes. He's not always so easily taken in by such nonsense, but it's worrying how vulnerable he can be.

'Would you like to go for a swim?' I ask Niall.

Niall is motionless, just staring out to the sea, but seconds later he dashes away from me and jumps into the water, fully clothed. It hasn't been a good day so far.

'Niall, please come back here,' I shout.

He simply laughs and starts kicking the water aimlessly, which doesn't amuse those near him. I swiftly strip down to my swimming trunks, and fetch him back to dry land.

I hear a few sniggers from a group of teenage girls nearby. I'm not sure whether it's for our antics, or the sight of me in speedos.

I remove his wet clothes and lay them on the beach. Although it's a nice day, I doubt that it'll become hot enough to dry them. I wonder how Kerry will react when Niall knocks on his front door wearing only his swimming trunks?

Niall then walks to the edge of the beach and stares out to sea. Both his hands are now clenched as fists and tucked under his chin. He has the expression of a person with the world's problems resting on his shoulders. I'd love to know what he's thinking.

Meanwhile Harry is running along the beach singing the signature tune of the cartoon television show *Scooby Do*. He has already asked several people if they like the show.

'Harry, you mustn't talk to strangers,' I say, as he skips towards me.

'But they're all my friends. That fat man over there told me that he doesn't have a telly, so I gave him our address and told him to come around to watch ours.'

'How many times have I told you about giving our address out to strangers? You mustn't do that again. You shouldn't talk to anyone that you don't know, and never go off with strangers, whatever they offer you.'

'But it's OK if someone gives me Skittles.'

'No it isn't. Only bad people will ask you to go with them, and they'll do horrible things to you.'

'What about Starbursts?'

'No, never go with strangers, is that clear?'

Harry looks at the sand and smiles.

'*Scooby Scooby Do where are you?*' he happily sings to himself, before running back into the sea.

Autistic children do not think logically in the same way as their peers. Most children will sooner or later grasp the seriousness of not talking to strangers, but Harry probably never will. That's why he needs supervision twenty-four hours a day, seven days a week. His only independence has to be in a safe environment, such as in his bedroom.

Soon afterwards my mobile rings; it's Laura.

How are you getting on?' she asks.

I immediately dismiss any thoughts of lying to her, as I'm certain that Harry will blab.

'It's been stressful.'

'Why? What have they been doing?'

'Niall ran across a busy road to get to a sweet shop. He almost got hit by a car.'

'Weren't you holding his hand?'

'Of course I was, but he's strong and quick.'

'You shouldn't have taken him.'

'Thanks for the morale booster, that's just what I need.'

'David, I'm sorry for giving you a hard time, but can't you see that I'm concerned about the boys?'

I don't respond.

'Have you told Kerry?' Laura asks.

'No, it'll only make her upset for the rest of the day. Laura, I better go, you know how Harry acts up when I'm on the phone.'

'How is he?'

'He's OK. I managed to convince him that the bees or wasps in Brighton don't sting.'

Laura isn't in the mood for any of my humour.

'Can I speak to him?'

She can probably hear him singing *Santa Claus is Coming to Town*. This song doesn't seem in sync with his surroundings, but Harry's build-up towards Christmas starts early. I hand the phone over to him.

'Harry, are you enjoying yourself?' Laura asks.

'Mum, the fat man wants to watch *Scooby Do* at our house.'

'What man are you talking about?'

'The fat man with hair coming out of his ears.'

The man in question is standing only a few feet away. I'm expecting a visit from him shortly.

'I'm glad that you're having a good time. Just remember to always stay close to Daddy, OK?'

Harry hands me back the phone before running back into the sea.

'Who's this man?'

'He's just a bloke on the beach that Harry got chatting to, no big deal.'

'I can't believe that you're letting him talk to strangers.'

'I was taking care of Niall at the time.'

Laura doesn't respond, which probably means that she's furious.

'Don't worry, they're both being good now.'

'Why don't you come back?'

'I'll give them a little longer on the beach before leaving.'

Laura mumbles a half-hearted response before hanging up.

I hope that my relationship with Laura isn't always going to be as stressful as this.

An hour later I'm feeling a little more relaxed. Harry is happily swimming only a few feet away from me, while Niall has been preoccupied with grabbing handfuls of sand, then patiently watching it filter through his fingers. Occasionally this gets him excited and he makes some strange grunting noises, but overall he's been well-behaved.

Seizing the quiet moment I decide to call Kerry.

'Kerry, it's David.'

'Hi, how's it going?'

'Good, they've both been fine, although Niall is a bit reluctant to go into the water.'

'Is he playing with the sand?'

'Yes, there isn't too much on this beach, but he's found enough to keep him focused for the past hour.'

'David, I'd love to speak more, but I've got to go back to class now. What time do you think you'll be back?'

'Around four.'

'Thanks so much for taking Niall, I appreciate it.'

Kerry hangs up. At two minutes past four she'll probably have me earmarked as both an irresponsible carer and a compulsive liar.

There is little interaction between Harry and Niall, but that's not unusual for Harry at least.

Harry joined an autistic pre school when he was five and up to that point he had no friends. His nursery classmates were divided in their opinion of my son; some were scared of him, while a couple of the more able boys mocked Harry for his strange behaviour.

One of his classmates, Peter, invited all of his class to his fifth birthday party; except Harry.

On a school summer fete I overheard a couple of woman describe Harry as a 'nut job' and 'has a screw loose'. I was saddened to hear such remarks and didn't pass on these kind words to Laura, given her fragile mental state.

That afternoon Harry confirmed their suspicions by knocking over the cake stand because the cakes were 'the wrong shape' and head butted a classmate because 'he shouldn't be wearing a yellow shirt'.

A couple of weeks after finding out he was autistic, our doctor informed us that he also has Attention Deficient Hyperactivity Disorder, which was not a surprise.

Although this was depressing news, it lead to Harry being prescribed Ritalin, which has helped to calm him down.

After a peaceful hour on the beach, I decide that it's time to leave.

'Come on, boys, we're going now.'

'Hurray, no more Brighton tossers to look at,' Harry shouts.

'Harry, you mustn't say that.'

'But London people aren't tossers.'

I hand Harry his towel.

'Can you dry yourself now?'

'Daddy, why don't you wear your swimming trunks to work?'

'I can't, I have to wear a suit.'

'Don't you ever want to swim in the London river?'

'It's called the River Thames. Did you learn that at school?'

'Mr Prick told us.'

'Harry, that's Mr Price, Anyway, the River Thames is too dirty to swim in.'

I've visions of walking to the embankment at lunchtime in my swimming trunks, and going in for a dip.

Meanwhile Niall is still staring out to the sea, so I approach him.

'Niall, we're going now.'

Without looking at me, Niall shakes his head. This surprises me, as it's the first appropriate response that I've seen from him.

'Shall we go to the clothes shop?'

Niall turns to face me and promptly spits in my face. He may not be able to speak, but he has no difficulty making his feelings known.

'Don't ever do that again, is that clear?' I shout, as I wipe the spit from my face.

Niall looks as if he's about to spit again, so I put my hand over his mouth.

'No spitting,' I say again, firmly.

I take my hand away and he immediately spits onto a nearby rock. I can faintly hear a middle-aged couple muttering something about the boy deserving a slap, but I don't want to get involved. I'm anxious to leave.

I tightly grip Niall's hand and start to make our way back to the promenade. Niall continues to show his frustration by head-butting me on my elbow several times. However, as soon as we leave the beach, he stops. Could this be his way of letting me know that he didn't want to leave?

Although Kerry had warned me yesterday about his spitting, I still find it extremely provoking and anti-social behaviour. Of course, Niall doesn't know any better.

We manage to find a sports shop within a short walking distance from the beach. Although Niall doesn't show the slightest interest in any of the clothes that I'm asking him to wear, at least he's co-operative. I eventually settle for dark blue shorts and a white shirt.

As we're walking back to the car, Harry is fixated on the sky again, in case of bee or wasp attacks. However, we arrive back in the car without any such attacks to Harry. There are also no further head-butts, spitting or suicide attempts from Niall.

I immediately play the Robbie Williams CD, which keeps the boys quiet throughout the journey. Niall is so busy listening to the music that he doesn't seem to notice when we drive past the same McDonalds that aroused such a spirited response earlier. I wonder if Robbie is aware how his music positively affects disabled children?

For the past half-an-hour I've been mentally rehearsing how to tell Kerry about Niall's near-death experience. I try to reassure myself that at least no one got hurt, but whatever words I manage to come up with cannot disguise the seriousness of the incident.

As we pull into Kerry's driveway Niall grits his teeth, before hitting his forehead with his fist.

'Hitting is finished,' I say. I'm assuming that he's excited to be home, but it's not easy to gauge his thoughts.

He then head-butts Harry's arm, to which Harry retaliates by elbowing the back of Niall's head.

'Harry, that's enough, you mustn't hurt Niall.'

'I don't care.'

'Well I do. I want you apologise to Niall.'

'But penguins can't fly.'

'That's irrelevant; now are you going to say sorry to Niall?'

'Sorry,' he reluctantly mumbles, 'now I'm going to look at all the Thomas stuff.'

Harry gets out of the car, just as Kerry approaches us. He rushes past her and into the house, without any acknowledgement. I glance at Niall, who has now calmed down.

'Niall, look it's your mum.'

Niall has been staring at his feet since Harry left, and doesn't look up at me or Kerry.

Kerry leans inside the car and immediately gives Niall a hug.

'I've missed you. Did you have a good day?'

Instead of looking at his mother, he extends the palm of his hand to me.

'Does he think I've got sweets?' I ask Kerry.

'I'm not sure. He's looking at your bag. Is his Action Man in there?'

'Of course.' I dig it out and hand it over to him.

Kerry unbuckles his seatbelt and takes his hand.

'David told me that you've been a good boy; well done.'

She triumphantly gives him the double thumbs up.

As soon as he steps onto the pavement, Niall breaks away from his mother and dashes into the house.

'He's always doing that,' Kerry remarks, with a wry smile. As if I didn't know.

'Kerry, I didn't tell you everything on the phone, hmm… as we were walking towards the beach…'

'Sorry, David, but I've just noticed Niall's clothes. Are they Harry's?'

'No, Niall jumped into the sea fully clothed and they didn't dry in time, so I just bought him some new ones on the way back.'

'You shouldn't have. Let me pay you.'

'Please don't, it's my treat.'

'No way; how much do I owe you?'

'Tell her now,' I repeat in my head, as we enter the house.

'Niall nearly got killed in Brighton, it was brilliant,' Harry shouts from the top of the stairs.

'OK, Harry, now go and play in the bedroom.'

Kerry stares at me. 'Is he joking?'

'I'm afraid not. As we were walking towards the beach Niall let go of my hand and ran across the road to try to get to a sweet shop. He missed getting run over only by a few inches. I feel terrible about this, I blame myself entirely.'

'Why didn't you tell me earlier?'

'I was about to, honestly. It happened as soon as we arrived in Brighton, but I didn't want to worry you.'

'You should've told me, David. I *am* his mother.'

'Of course, but I'm sure that you'd have told me to come straight back, and Niall would've been disappointed. Apart from jumping in the sea fully-clothed, the rest of the day went fine.'

Kerry slumps into a kitchen chair, 'I can't take any more of this.'

She rests her head in her hands and shakes her head repeatedly. An awkward silence lingers for a few minutes, before Kerry speaks again.

'Why doesn't he ever do as he's told? He's been warned so many times about doing that and I thought that I'd seen the last of it. The problem is there's no easy solution. What should I do? Handcuff him to me every time we go out?'

'If he's doing it less than before, he'll probably stop it sooner or later.'

'I hope so. He's getting quicker and stronger and I'm getting older. Maybe the next driver won't be so alert.'

Kerry gets up and fills the kettle. 'Do you fancy a cuppa?'

'Shall we have something a bit stronger?' I produce a bottle of red wine out of the wet clothes bag. 'It's a peace offering.'

'David, he's done this to me and others before, so how can I blame you for anything? You were kind enough to look after him and it couldn't have been easy having Harry with you as well. No, I'm grateful to you.'

'Thanks; now where's the corkscrew?'

An hour later and Kerry seems more relaxed, probably due to the wine consumption.

'David, I'm sorry for getting upset earlier. There are some days when everything gets too much for me.'

'You don't have to apologise, it must be a big worry for you.'

'Yes, but I'm sure that you've got enough problems of your own.'

'Do you think Danny's departure has affected Niall's behaviour?'

'Thanks for mentioning that arsehole's name, that's lifted my spirits no end.'

'I'm sorry, I didn't mean to …'

'I'm only joking. Niall's behaviour hasn't changed significantly since Danny left. I've no idea how much he thinks about his dad.'

'How did you find out about the affair?'

'Danny always went down the pub once or twice a week with his mates, but he was staying out more and more and coming home less drunk every time. One day I looked at his mobile bill and kept seeing the same number cropping up again and again, so I rang it.'

'What did you say?'

'A woman answered it. I recognised her voice straight away. I had met Sheryl at Danny's office Christmas party. She's attractive and all the blokes, including Danny, were all over her. I accused the trollop of having an affair with Danny and she admitted it, without hesitation. He moved out a couple of days later, and I haven't heard from him since. Three months without seeing his son; what a great father.'

Harry bursts into the living room, wearing Niall's pyjamas. The top is on the wrong way around, so that the buttons are on his back.

'Harry, why are you wearing Niall's pyjamas?'

'Because mine are too far away.'

'Why don't you take the pyjamas off, we're going soon.'

'But Niall's bedroom has *Toy Story* wallpaper, so I have to stay; I want to stare at Buzz Lightyear all night long.'

'David, why don't you stay? Niall's got bunk beds, so that's no problem and you can sleep in the spare room.'

'Thanks, but we should go home.'

'You can't drive after the wine and as you're not working tomorrow, what's the rush?'

'Oh come on, Daddy, this house is magic. It has nineteen *Thomas* DVDs and there's no bats.'

Bats are another one of Harry's phobias.

'Well the fact that this house has no bats is the deciding factor. Yes, we'd love to stay.'

'In that case you can help me finish off this bottle,' Kerry responds, as she pours me another glass.

'Our milkman comes between five minutes past six and eighteen minutes past six. What time does your milkman arrive?' Harry asks Kerry.

'I don't know.'

'That's OK. I'll be up at five o'clock, so I don't miss him. How many bottles do you have?'

'Two. Why?'

'I have to check that he's doing his job correctly. I sometimes open the front door when he's walking up our path, to count the number of bottles that he puts down.'

'That's very thorough of you.'

'Well if he miscalculates, it'll be disastrous. Daddy likes two Weetabixes for breakfast and has lots of cups of tea or coffee, but I don't like milk.'

'OK, Harry, I think that you've exhausted the milkman story. Why don't you go up to Niall's room and settle down for the night?'

'Does Niall like to stay awake at night?' Harry asks.

'Sometimes, but I think tonight he'll be sleeping.'

'Harry, you must not play your DVDs in the middle of the night because it'll wake up Niall,' I tell him.

'But what else is there to do?'

'You need to sleep, otherwise you'll get ill.'

'Cool, puking up is fun. Last week Matthew vomited all over Mrs Law's dress and we all laughed. Mrs Law didn't look happy though.'

'Can you put on your pyjamas the right way around and then go up to bed?'

Harry rushes upstairs, obviously delighted.

The noise from Niall's bedroom gradually fades during the next half an hour.

'David, I've enjoyed this evening, although I feel guilty for talking about myself too much,' Kerry remarks, as we both drink the last of the wine.

'Don't worry about it. It's therapeutic to listen to other people's problems.'

'I think I'll head off to bed. Come on let me show you the spare room.'

I follow her upstairs and pop into Niall's room to find that Harry is now fast asleep.

The sea air has done its job.

The house is quiet. It's a peaceful ending to what has been a stressful day.

Redundancy

Nine hours later I wake up. I immediately jump out of bed and run into Niall's bedroom, which is empty. I rush downstairs to find both Niall and Harry tucking into their Rice Krispies, with no milk. Kerry, opposite them, is drinking coffee.

'Good morning. Coffee?' she asks.

'Yes, please. Harry, what time did you get up?'

'Four fifty-seven and the milkman came at five thirty-two. He delivered two bottles of milk. I congratulated him for getting it right.'

'You were talking to the milkman?'

'Of course. I was waiting for him.'

'Don't worry, David, I was there too,' Kerry explains.

'Why didn't you wake me up?'

'I thought that you were in need of a good night's sleep. The milkman was a bit bemused when Harry started to talk to him, especially when he asked if he'd broken any bottles this week.'

'Well, had he?'

'He said five, so Harry told him to be more careful in future. I had to explain Harry's autism to him.'

'What time did you get up?' I ask Kerry.

'I heard Harry go downstairs, so I followed him.'

'Oh I'm sorry, Kerry. What was he doing?'

'Looking for sweets.'

'Daddy, I couldn't find any Starbursts or Skittles, there was only a Crunchie bar, which tasted like dog's turd.'

'But you still ate it?'

'I took a bite, but spat it out all over Niall's mum.'

'You did what?'

'David, don't worry, I'm used to it with Niall's spitting.'

'Did you apologise to Kerry?'

'What's the point?'

'What do you mean, what's the point? It's rude to spit at people.'

'But Niall spat eight times yesterday, and I didn't want that Crunchie shit in my mouth.'

'Harry, I'm not going to ask you again.'

'David, there's no need,' Kerry remarks.

'You see, she isn't bothered, but why did she have that Crunchie there in the first place?'

'Harry, if you don't apologise now I'm going to take away all of your Thomas DVDs as soon as we get back home.'

'OK, sorry, but why are you blaming me? It's all Batman's fault.'

'Of course it is.'

'The next time I come here, you've got to have Starbursts,' Harry demands, before running upstairs. I'm about to call him down again before Kerry interrupts.

'David, I was only wearing a crappy tee-shirt, it's already been washed clean, so why don't you sit down and I'll make you that coffee.'

I sit next to Niall, who is happily eating his Rice Krispies.

'Are you enjoying your breakfast?' I ask, but Niall continues to eat without even glancing at me.

'I'm afraid he's very focused on food,' Kerry confesses.

The moment Kerry hands me my coffee Niall grabs my cup and takes a swill.

'I see that he likes coffee.'

'Niall drinks everything – tea, coffee, beer, wine, even whisky. Whenever we have a family gathering here, he'll drink all afternoon.'

'Does he ever get sick?'

'No, you'd think that mixture of alcohol will help him sleep though, but it doesn't,' Kerry explains, with an ironic expression.

'Is there anything that he won't drink?'

'No. A couple of months ago I read on the Internet about an autistic girl who was continually spitting. As a deterrent, the girl's mother gave her a spoonful of malt vinegar every time she spat, and the girl eventually stopped. So I tried the same with Niall, but he actually liked the taste of vinegar so much that he kept drinking it straight from the bottle when I wasn't looking. In the end I gave up and hid the vinegar bottle.'

Niall finishes his Rice Krispies, then takes my hand and leads me to a drawer above the cooker. As it's too high for him to reach, he pushes my hand in the direction of the handle.

'Niall, no sweets.' Kerry tells her son. Niall runs over to the glass-panelled kitchen door and kicks one of the panels, breaking the glass into hundreds of small pieces. Luckily he is wearing trainers.

Kerry rushes to Niall to check that he isn't hurt, but soon realises that only the glass is broken.

'Niall, that was naughty. Go into the living room and sit quietly.'

Kerry shakes her head, as she brushes up the glass. 'Why is he so destructive?'

'Harry has done this a few times, so I've repaired a lot of panels. If you can give me a tape measure, I'll work out the dimensions of the glass and order you another one today. I'll come back to fix it on for you, if that's OK?'

'Oh, David, thanks so much. I'm crap at DIY.' Kerry says, as she empties the broken glass into the bin.

'At least I won't be contacting the home insurance people this time. We're almost on first name terms after all the things that Niall has broken. In the past two months alone, he's smashed the television screen, broken our bed by using it as a trampoline and pulled the cooker door off its hinges.'

I follow Kerry into the living room, where we find Niall sitting on a sofa playing with an Action Man, who has only a torso and a pair of legs.

'Niall, look at the damage you did to the door,' Kerry says.

Niall continues to prod his Action Man, so Kerry gently turns him around to face the door.

'You mustn't do that again, do you hear me?'

Niall now seems to be focused on the wall opposite him, so Kerry brings him closer to the door.

'Niall, looking,' Kerry points her forefinger near his eyes and then at the door. This time Niall looks at the glass panel, minus the glass. He kneels down and puts his hand through the empty panel several times, smiling as he does so.

'Does he understand that he's doing wrong?'

'Sometimes, but I'm afraid most of the time he hasn't got a clue why I'm reprimanding him.'

Niall walks out of the living room and then runs upstairs.

'Niall, can you bring down your training shoes please?' Kerry shouts.

A short time later he returns, shoes in hand.

'That's impressive,' I say.

'About three months ago he started to understand some very simple sentences, which I'm absolutely thrilled about.'

Kerry kneels down to tie Niall's shoelaces, while he continues to pull the legs of his beheaded and armless Action Man. She holds Niall's hand and heads towards the front door.

'Is it OK if I come back tomorrow to fix the glass?' I ask.

'Of course,' Kerry says.

'We'll be leaving soon after you. I'll make sure that Harry doesn't stuff any more Thomas DVDs down his underpants.'

'Thanks again for taking care of the door,' Kerry smiles, before leaving the house.

I decide to pop upstairs to see what Harry's up to. I find him lying on Niall's bed, reading the telephone directory, which is another one of his favourite pastimes.

'Come on, Harry, put the directory away, we're going now.'

'Daddy, this is the two thousand and fifteen directory for South London.'

'That's great.'

'But we only have the two thousand and fourteen one, so can I take this?'

'No, don't take anything that belongs to Niall's mother, is that clear?'

At least he can't stuff the telephone directory in his underpants.

'But why haven't we got it?'

'I don't know. Why are you always looking at it anyway?'

'I want to check out all the Streatham addresses.' Streatham is where we live.

'The first time I checked the directory I found three hundred and sixteen, but I wanted to double-check this, so the second time I found three hundred and nineteen.'

'Just as well you double-checked then. Now tidy up Niall's room and we'll go.'

I go downstairs to wash a few dishes, while waiting for Harry.

A short time later he comes charging down the stairs and jumps down the last half a dozen of them.

'Hold on a second, let me check you.'

'But I haven't got any stuff.'

I give him a through body search, even removing his underpants to check for any DVDs.

'That's a good boy, Harry, no stealing this time.'

'*Now* can I have the Thomas' *Snowy Surprise* DVD?'

'You know the answer to that, let's go.'

Though Harry's disappointed, within a few minutes in the car he sings all the Thomas classics – 'He's A Really Useful Engine', 'It's Great To Be An Engine', 'James The Splendid Engine' and 'Percy's Seaside Trip'.

Sometimes I find myself singing the Thomas songs when I'm alone, in much the same way that you sing along to an irritating, but catchy, pop song that you constantly hear on the radio.

I park outside our house.

'This time it only took thirteen minutes and six seconds, but yesterday morning it took twenty-one minutes and thirty-two seconds, so well done, Daddy.'

'That's probably because we travelled during the rush hour yesterday,' I mention, but Harry is already getting out of the car, obviously not interested in the variables.

Mrs Connelly, my next-door neighbour, approaches me.

'How are you, David?'

'Good, and yourself?'

'I can't complain. The arthritis plays me up more these days, but it's worse in the winter. How's Laura?'

'She's doing well.'

'She's not cracking up again?'

'No, she's fit and healthy.'

'And what about young Harry – is he getting any better?'

'He's fine.'

'It's such a shame. In years gone by they'd have put him in an institution and thrown away the key, so I do admire you for bringing him up yourself, it can't be easy.'

'It's not too bad.'

'OK, you take care and tell Laura to pop in for a cup of tea, the poor love.'

'I will.'

I quickly open the front door and into the safety of our house.

'Nosey old cow,' I mutter.

'I don't think she looks like a cow, but her face does remind me of a pig though,' Harry remarks.

Usually I'd reprimand him for such a comment, but this morning I can't help but smile.

'Daddy, you left your phone in the car last night. Mummy has left four messages for you,' Harry tells me, as he hands me my mobile.

I simply forgot to contact Laura when we got back to Kerry's house. I also notice that there are three messages on the house phone. I decide to ring her at work.

'Oh hi, Laura, I'm sorry about not contacting you last night.'

'Well you've finally got back to me. I was going to throttle you yesterday. I kept ringing you and after getting your answering machine for the umpteenth time, I started to worry. I decided to drive to the house and wait there, as I didn't know what else to do, but when I passed Kerry's house I saw your car parked outside. I was half thinking about popping in to give you a mouthful, but it wouldn't have been appropriate. So did you stay the night?'

'Yes I did. We had some wine, so I thought it was safer not to drive.'

'Good, that was wise. How did Harry sleep?'

'OK, he got up at around five to check out the milkman.'

'Did he talk to him?'

'I wasn't up, but he did ask the milkman about his broken bottles.'

'You weren't awake? Was he on his own?'

'No, Kerry was with him. She got up when she heard him go downstairs. She also made his breakfast and let me have a sleep in.'

'Wasn't that kind of her?' Laura adds, with a hint of sarcasm.

'Shouldn't you be happy that she looked after Harry?' I ask.

'I'm sorry, you're right. I suppose it's hard thinking about you having a relationship with another woman.'

'Having a relationship? I just took her son out for the day, I'm not going to order the wedding cake just yet. Besides, she's married.'

'Barely. So, what did she say about Niall's accident?'

'She was upset, but it's happened before so it wasn't a surprise to her. I'll ring you later.'

'OK,' Laura quietly replies.

I place the telephone back on its hook and play the first phone message.

'Hi, David, I just wanted to know how you got on, give me a call when you get in.'

I press the delete button and play the next message, which is recorded thirty minutes later.

'I'm getting a bit concerned now, I'll try your mobile.'

I immediately delete this message and play the last one

'David, it's Alison Foster from HR. I know that you're on leave at the moment, but there have been some major developments on the restructuring plans that I need to discuss with you. Can you ring me back please? My extension is 6211. Thanks.'

Everyone knows that another company restructuring is imminent, but up to now I haven't been too con-cerned. I've survived three restructures already, so why should this one be any different? However, I wouldn't receive a phone call from the head of personnel unless it's something serious. The message is brief and to the point, very business-like. The tone in her voice indicates that it's not good news, but there's only one way to find out.

I dial her number. 'Alison, it's David McCarthy.'

'Thanks for getting back to me, David. We now know more details on the restructuring plans, and how this affects you.'

'Am I being made redundant?'

'I can't discuss this over the phone. I know that you live close to the office, so is it possible you can come in?'

'You can't tell me whether I've a job to go to next week?'

'I'd rather talk about this face-to-face. What time can you get here?'

'In about half-an-hour.'

'That's fine, please go straight to my office.'

'OK,' I mutter.

I rush upstairs to have a quick wash and shave, although I'm not sure if turning up clean-shaven will be the deciding factor in saving my job.

'Come on, Harry, I need to see someone at work.'

'But *Bugs Bunny* is on in five minutes.'

'Fuck *Bugs Bunny*, now let's get moving.'

'Good swearing, Dad.'

'Just record it, so you can watch it when we get back.'

I instantly regret swearing, as I've spent the last few months discouraging Harry from doing so. He'll remember this for at least the next twenty years. Harry sets the TiVo cable box and a few minutes later we're on our way to Homely Insurance. I've worked for this company for thirteen years. Prior to this job I was a postman, but the combination of going out in the cold, rainy days and listening to the punters forever moaning about missing letters, convinced me that I needed a career break, preferably with a job indoors. My friend Steve, who works in IT, encouraged me to attend evening classes to study computer science. Eighteen months later, after passing my exams, I landed the position of computer programmer at Homely Insurance. The first year or two were exciting as I was learning new skills, but for the past decade I've been bored. Still, I think that I'm good at my job and am now the most experienced programmer in our department.

It takes us only ten minutes to get to Homely Insurance, and as we're going up in the lift, Harry presses all the buttons for the other floors. The two senior managers who replace us in the lift, will have a longer journey than usual, as they both work on the fourteenth floor.

Alison is on the phone. She beckons us in.

'Linda, thanks for the update, I've got a meeting right now but I'll ring you back in about ten minutes.'

Ten minutes – is that all I get for thirteen years of service?

'Thanks very much for coming in, David,' she proclaims, giving me a painted smile.

I nod.

'As you know we're going through a restructuring period and I'm afraid that your role was identified in the jobs at risk group.'

'I'm being made redundant. Am I right?'

'Yes you are, I'm afraid.'

'But I've got more systems knowledge than most people in the company, so why me?'

'The company needs to cut down its IT department by twenty per cent,' she proclaims.

'Is it because of my age?'

'You know that we are an equal opportunities company, so that'll never be an issue. However, I cannot divulge the reasons why it was decided to let you go. David, I know that this is a shock to you, but we've come up with a generous redundancy package, that I hope you'll be pleased with.'

She hands me a piece of paper that confirms my leaving date will be in four weeks time and a redundancy amount of twenty-eight thousand, five hundred and two pounds and seventy-eight pence. It's a huge sum of money, but how long will it last if I don't get another job quickly?

Suddenly this horrendous smell engulfs the room. Harry has broken wind.

'Stop doing that,' I whisper to him.

'But that's my life.'

'Don't break wind again. If you need to go to the toilet, just tell me.'

The last time I said this to him we did indeed go to the toilet, where he took his trousers down and farted over the toilet bowl. He then put his trousers back on, washed his hands and left.

Alison grimaces as the scent of Harry's fart finally reaches her.

'I'm sorry about that, he has a gastro problem,' I explain to her.

His lack of social skills means that he doesn't feel any inhibitions in breaking wind any time or place. Last month he did it on a crowded bus and the teenage couple sitting behind us started having an argument, as the girl thought that her boyfriend was the culprit. 'That is evil', were the last words she spoke to him before leaving the bus on her own. I hope that their relationship will overcome Harry's indiscretion.

It takes a few minutes for the smell to recede. I'm about to ask Alison a question, but Harry beats me to it.

'How many times do you fart during the day?'

'David, I hope that you don't mind me saying this, but this is a place of business and your son should act appropriately.'

'I apologise for his behaviour, but if you've actually looked through my personnel file you'll see that my son is autistic. I know that it must be noted somewhere, as his autism is the reason why I get to work from home. Unfortunately, Harry will hardly ever act appropriately.'

For the first time since the meeting started Alison doesn't seem in control, as she frantically looks up my details on her computer.

'Oh yes, please accept my apologies.'

'Do I need to sign this document to make everything official?'

'Yes, but you can take it away and sign it in your own time. When I get it back I'll make a copy of it for you.'

'What if I don't sign it?'

'Then you may end up loosing your job without any severance payment.'

'It seems as if I've got little option then.'

I take a pen out of my jacket pocket and immediately sign the form, before handing it back to Alison.

'Do you happen to know any companies that want a forty-two-year old computer programmer, who also has sole custody of a twelve-year-old autistic child, whose needs on some days, take precedence over his job?'

'David, I'm sorry about this. I'm sure you'll find another position soon enough,' she trots out the standard, well-rehearsed reply, as she photocopies my documented day of execution.

I look at her and just nod, as I don't feel like talking.

'Paul Norris rang earlier, he wants to see you, if you've got the time,' Alison says, as she hands me the copied version of my redundancy notice. My ten minutes has now been reduced to five, but I've no doubt that she has to go though this many more times today.

'OK.'

'I know that this is not good news, but we didn't want to wait until Monday, when most people in the building would've known about it.'

To say that this is not good news is quite an understatement. I can only think of three worst experiences in my life – my father's death, divorcing Laura and finding out that Harry is autistic.

Just as we're walking out of the room, Harry turns around to look at Alison.

'I think you fart about five times a day.'

Alison looks bemused; it's obvious that she's an ambitious, career person, who doesn't have any children. I'm sure that the last five minutes experience with Harry won't exactly change her mind about having babies. This time I can't be bothered to apologise and instead of taking the lift, we make our way towards the emergency steps to meet up with Paul, who's my manager.

'Do you know what that lady was saying to me?' I ask Harry, as we start to walk down the stairs.

'She gave you a piece of paper.'

'Do you know what was on that paper?'

'Stories.'

'No, it was telling me I don't work here anymore. Do you know what that means?'

'That we can leave now?'

'It means I won't have much money.'

'Then just go to the bank, they'll give you some money.'

'Yes of course, that's what I'll do.'

I quickly walk past several colleagues, before reaching Paul's office. I feel embarrassed and sense that they feel awkward too. Paul gets up to greet us.

'Thanks for popping down; can you shut the door please?'

'Paul, this is Harry.'

'Good to meet you,' Paul says, as he shakes his hand.

'What's up, doc?' Harry says.

'He's into Bugs Bunny at the moment,' I explain.

'David, I'm sorry to hear the news, I honesty didn't know until yesterday afternoon. I was told not to contact you until the official announcement was made today.'

'Paul, what was your input into all of this?'

'Very little, I just had to supply personnel with a list of names in my team, their skill set and experience. My opinion on each individual was never asked, although they did look at the annual review documents. Your review was excellent, so I'm surprised that they chose you.'

'Your hair looks just like Bruce Forsyth's,' Harry suddenly blurts out.

Paul looks at Harry, but doesn't respond. He wears a hair-piece, but nobody has ever mentioned this to him; until now.

'I love it when Bruce says "nice to see you, to see you nice". Isn't he just fantastic?'

'Yes, he's a good entertainer.'

'I liked him best in *Play Your Cards Right*. It's on UK Gold on Saturday and Sunday afternoons at five o'clock. He only worked twenty-two minutes per week when he was on that show, because of the eight minutes commercials, and then sixty minutes per week in *Strictly Come Dancing*. Why didn't you take over from Brucie when he left *Strictly*?'

'Harry, please be quiet. I have to talk to Paul.'

'But why is his hair a different colour at the top of his head, to the hair near his ears?' Harry asks.

'Harry, if you speak again I'm not going to buy you any sweets on the way home.'

Harry doesn't reply, but keeps on staring at Paul's hair. One day I may laugh about all of this, but not today.

'I'm sorry about that, he doesn't mean to be offensive, it's just …'

'David, there's no need to explain; I understand.'

'What am I going to do about getting a job? The IT industry want young graduates, who are willing to bring their beds into work and spend every waking moment there. I've got a lot of commitments outside of work.'

'David, please don't despair, you're an excellent programmer and I'll be happy to give you an outstanding reference.'

'There's a few programmers out there who are crap. Are they going?' I say, pointing to my ex-colleagues.

'You're the only one from our department leaving.'

'When was the last time Bob wrote a program that actually worked? Did you tell personnel that?'

'As I said, my input was on your review.'

'I'm sorry, Paul, I shouldn't be angry with you. I better go. I'll see you on Monday.'

I shake Paul's hand, before leaving his office.

'Not such good news then?' Ashley asks me, as I'm walking past his desk. Ashley is a team colleague of mine.

'I've had better days.' I'm anticipating a response from Ashley, but he merely stares at me, so I start to walk away.

'Did you fix that registry problem on your PC?' Ashley enquires.

'Yes, I followed all of your system restore steps and it worked.'

'Good, when you come in on Monday, I'll let you know how to partition your hard drive, so if it happens again, you'll have some back-up.'

'Thanks.'

'Are you one of those pricks that Daddy is always talking about?' Harry asks Ashley.

Ashley looks confused, but doesn't respond.

Working with computer programmers is a strange experience. Most of them are extremely clever, but their passion and knowledge in life extends mainly to computers. Their social skills are virtually non-existent. Our Christmas party every year is like a visit to the morgue. The conversation is painful, any reference to anything other than computers is met with silence. 'Where do you live?', 'how do you get into work?', 'what university did you go to?', 'are you going abroad this summer?' are typical of the inane questions that I often ask and am not the slightest bit interested in the reply. I suspect my leaving do won't exactly be the social event of the year. This team have got embarrassing silences down to a fine art.

Soon after we leave the office I dial Laura's mobile.

'Laura, I've got some bad news.'

'Is Harry OK?'

'He's fine. I just found out that I'm being made redundant,' I blurt out.

'You're joking, right?'

'Would I joke about something like that?'

'But you were so confident this time around.'

'I was wrong, what can I say?'

'I can't believe it. When's your last day?'

'In four weeks.'

'What are you going to do about finding another job?'

'I only found out ten minutes ago, so I haven't had much time to think about it yet.'

'Why don't you come around tonight and we'll talk about it.'

'OK, I'll speak to you later.'

'Are we going to McDonalds?' Harry asks.

'No.'

'BurgerKing?'

'No.'

'OK, it has to be KFC.'

'No, we're going home, I'll cook you something there.'

'But that's boring; can't we go to the shops?'

'Not today, I need time to think.'

'Can't you think when I'm having my fries in McDonalds?'

I shake my head.

Fifteen minutes later I'm drinking a cup of tea in the kitchen, while Harry is watching the Mel Brooks DVD

Spaceballs in German. I'm pleased that, for once, he's watching something more age appropriate, but in German?

When Harry was six, Homely Insurance decided to have a kids at work day. Being an equal opportunities employer they insisted that I bring Harry along, despite my reservations. They would live to regret that decision.

All the work parents and their children gathered in the atrium and the co-ordinator asked the kids to say something about themselves. When it was Harry's turn he said 'this floor is rubbish, it makes too much noise.' To prove his point he walked back and forth for a couple of minutes. 'And my Dad told his friend last week that the old good thing about this joint is Susan Moore's tits.'

'OK, let's move on,' was all a shocked co-ordinator could say.

After the introductions we were then shown a DVD of the history of Homely Insurance. How even the most dedicated employee would struggle to get through this, and of course Harry didn't take too kindly to it.

'Shut the fuck up, you boring piece of shit,' Harry shouted at the screen.

'I think that you were probably correct in your initial assessment of your son's suitability for this activity. Why don't you take the day off and put it down as approved absence?' A scared looking lady from personnel pleaded with me.

I've never been told to get lost in such a polite way, but it took several apologies before my work colleague Susan would speak to me again.

'Daddy, I want to invite Robert to my house.' Robert is Harry's school friend.

'OK, do you have his telephone number?'

Harry immediately dials Robert's number and after spending the first few minutes talking about Percy the green engine, he eventually asks him to come over. I speak briefly to his mother, who tells me that she'll be over shortly. They only live a five-minute drive away.

'They're here,' Harry excitedly announces half-an-hour later. He rushes to the front door to let them in.

I recognise Robert's mother, Stephanie, from various school events.

'Thanks, David, for offering to look after Robert. He's so pleased to be with Harry.'

'No problem. What time will you be coming back?' I hope that didn't sound too pushy.

'By about four, I've got a date tonight and I want to buy some new clothes.'

'I hope he's worth it.'

'It looks promising. He's the keep fit instructor at the local gym, so I don't think we'll be discussing world politics, if you know what I mean.'

'Yes I do,' I say, feeling embarrassed in getting involved in a mildly sexual conversation with someone that I hardly know.

'Robert, be a good boy for David, and I'll see you at four.'

She gives Robert a kiss and says her goodbyes, before driving off to the nearest designer clothes shop.

I shut the door and when I turn around Robert is standing right in front of me.

'My name is Robert, that's R – O – B – E – R – T. My dad's name is William, that's W – I – L – L – I – A – M. Some people call him Bill, my mum calls him a bastard. Daddy doesn't live with us anymore. He lives in the postcode southwest eight, two, N, A. Do you like my mummy?'

'Yes, I do.'

'She has a lot of men friends, they sleep at our house sometimes.'

'That's nice.'

'Whenever a man talks to Mummy they don't look at her face, they just stare at her breasts. Why do they do that?'

'I'm not sure.'

'Maybe they want to shag their willies,' Harry adds.

'OK, Harry, don't talk like that in front of Robert.'

'Do you like butter?' Robert asks me.

'Well, yes I suppose.'

'When Mummy's not looking I like to eat the butter from the tub. Do you do that?'

'No, I just like it in a sandwich.'

'That's gross,' Robert screeches, in an American accent.

Whenever I'm around Harry's classmates at his school, they all tend to speak to each other in American accents, as they regurgitate lines of dialogue from an American film or cartoon.

'Do you want anything to eat?'

'Yes, can I have pizza, chips, beans and lemonade?'

'Well done, Robert, that's a bloody perfect dinner. Give me the same, Daddy.'

'Have you got any brown sauce?' Robert asks.

'Yes, Harry likes it.'

'Fantastic, pizza is crap without the brown sauce.'

As I place the defrosted pizza in the oven I look out to the garden and see Figaro sitting on our trampoline. Like all cats, she has a simplistic lifestyle. She doesn't have to worry about mortgages, the poll tax or any utility bills. Once Figaro's fed, she's content and then sleeps for the rest of the day. Why can't my life be like that?

'Robert, spit it out now,' I hear Harry shout.

I rush into the living room. 'What's the problem?'

'Robert's eating my *Spaceballs* DVD cover.'

Robert is indeed chewing paper and as a portion of the DVD cover is missing, I'm assuming it's in his mouth. I immediately take the non-chewed cover off Robert and hand it back to Harry.

'What am I going to do now? This DVD is destroyed.'

'It's only part of the cover, you can still watch the DVD.'

'What's the point?' Harry takes the DVD out and tosses it into the rubbish bin.

'Why did he eat my cover? Daddy, can't you give him *The Sun* to eat?'

'No, I'm not giving him any newspapers.'

Harry went through a phase of eating paper. When I say a phase, it lasted nearly three years, it was mainly newspapers, he seemed to prefer *The Sun* to the *Daily Mail*. I take the DVD out of the bin.

'Harry, I'll get you another *Spaceballs* DVD tomorrow, is that OK?'

'Can you get me the spaced-out edition? It has a second DVD of extras.'

'Yes, I suppose so.'

That paper-chewing act by Robert has just cost me fifteen pounds.

I spend the next half an hour doing various household chores in the kitchen and dining room. The only voice that I can hear from the living room is Bugs

Bunny's. Isn't it amazing that the cartoons that gave me so much enjoyment as a child are still as popular today?

I grab a can of Coke from the fridge and venture into the garden. The prospect of redundancy is dominating my thoughts. As part of the divorce settlement I bought out Laura's share of the house, leaving me with a huge mortgage. Consequently, I can't afford to take a big drop in salary.

I also have to remain in the Streatham area for Harry's school. Selling and buying another property in a cheaper area is not an option, as Harry is happy in his school and there isn't exactly an abundance of autistic schools to choose from.

It's at these emotional times that I wish my dad was still around to reassure me that everything will be OK. When he passed away four years ago from lung cancer, I was devastated. He was everything that I could wish for in a father – strong, gentle, kind, funny and loving. I still think about him most days. He was from the old school, that didn't fully understand autism. He always kept telling me that 'he'll grow out of it,' I gave up saying that he wouldn't. Dad and Harry were very close and when Dad died I dreaded telling Harry that his grandfather had gone to heaven. He cried for about a week, but rarely mentions him now.

Dad died before I divorced Laura, and I vividly remember a dream that I had during the divorce proceedings. I went to stay at the family cottage in Cork, Ireland, to get away from everything. Dad appeared as a ghost and gently helped me through this troubled time in my life.

I remember so clearly the conversations that I had with him in my dream, letting him know how much I loved him. I wished I had told him that when he was alive. When I woke up and realised that it was only a dream, I cried more than I did on the day of his funeral.

Although I've always got on reasonably well with my mother, I've never been as close to her. My parents had a happy marriage and she desperately misses him. I'll visit her tomorrow, but I won't tell her about the redundancy, as she worries so much. I'll wait until I get another job.

As I've been in the garden now for over five minutes, I decide to go back inside and check on the boys. I walk into the living room, and although Bugs Bunny is still chattering away, Harry and Robert are nowhere to be seen. I rush out to the hallway where the sight of an open front door immediately sends me into a panic. I shout their names, but there's no response.

I stand outside the house and listen for any sound of Harry, but all that greets me is silence. I go inside to check all the rooms, but they've left the house. They must have gone to the shops. I grab the car keys and within seconds I'm driving to the nearest shops, which are only a few minutes' walk away.

As Harry hasn't tried to escape from the house for such a long time, I can only assume that this is Robert's idea. They can't have gone too far, as I was only in the garden a short time, but what shop will they go into first, if indeed they have gone to the shops? The first shop I see is WH Smiths. I dash across the road and practically take the hinges off the door, but after frantically running up and down the aisles, I cannot find them.

A few shops away is HMV. As usual it's crowded, which makes it difficult to manoeuvre quickly between the customers. I brush into a few people, but don't bother to apologise.

I approach the security guard.

'Excuse me, I've lost my son and his friend, can you help me look for them please?' I ask desperately.

'What do they look like?' The security guard responds.

I describe them to him and for the next few minutes we search the entire store, all to no avail.

'Do you want me to call the police?'

I shake my head and rush out of the store, without thanking him. If I don't find them quickly, I'll have to make that phone call.

Now I'm panicking. What if they didn't make it to the shops and were picked up instead? I feel physically sick at the thought of this nightmare scenario.

Have they gone into the sweet shop? It's a couple of hundred yards away from HMV, so I run as fast as I can, and by the time I reach it I'm out of breath.

I open the door and see about a dozen people queuing up, and the two people at the top of the queue are Harry and Robert.

'Oh, thank God,' I say a little too loudly, as several people turn around and stare at me. They must think I'm some sort of a religious nut.

I rush to the front of the queue.

'What the hell do you think you're doing, leaving the house without telling me?' I shout at Harry.

'Excuse me, are these your kids?' The shopkeeper asks me.

'Yes. Why?'

'Because their sweets cost three pounds and thirty pence and they've only giving me seven pence and they keep asking for change back.'

I look onto the counter and see two packets of Starbursts, one packet of Skittles, a Milky Way and inevitably a *Thomas the Tank Engine* magazine.

'Could you pay the man please? We've been waiting here for ages,' shouts a lady in the queue.

I can sense that the queue is restless, so I immediately pay the shopkeeper.

'About bloody time, you'd think that they're old enough to work out that seven pence is less than three pounds and thirty pence,' a middle-aged man loudly announces.

'I'm sorry that you had to wait, but these two kids are autistic and don't understand the value of money.'

'If they're autistic, then why are they on their own?'

'What do you mean, *if* they are autistic?'

The man's attention is diverted, as he has to pay for his newspapers. I use this opportunity to leave the shop.

I deliberately avoided the man's question about why Harry and Robert were unaccompanied, because I know that this is all my fault. I shouldn't have gone out to the garden and left the boys alone in the house.

'So, why did you leave the house without telling me?' I ask, as we're walking towards the car.

'We needed sweets,' Harry replies.

'But you should've told me first, you're not allowed out on your own.'

'Popeye does it, so why can't we?' Robert chips in.

'Leave Popeye out of this. I'll say it one last time. Do *not* leave the house on your own. Is that clear?'

They simply stare at me. Tears start to fall down my cheek, so I quickly wipe them away.

'Daddy, why are you crying?'

I'm too emotional to respond.

'You must have a belly ache, and that's because you haven't cooked our dinner yet.'

I nod, as I try to regain some composure, on our way back to the car.

'Daddy, isn't it great having Robert at our house?'

'Yeah,' I reply, not too convincingly.

Five minutes later we're back in the house, with the front door now fully bolted and all the door keys in my pocket.

Within twenty minutes we're all sitting down at the dinner table having our pizzas. I've added some broccoli, so at least some of the meal is healthy.

'Broccoli is bollocks,' Robert shouts, as he throws his portion in the rubbish bin.

'Now you're talking my language,' Harry adds.

Robert then spends the next few minutes meticulously picking out the tiny specs of broccoli that have landed on his pizza, before he starts his meal.

'Mr McCarthy, where's Mrs McCarthy?' Robert enquires.

'We're divorced, she lives in a different house.'

'The only people I know that are still married are Edith and George. They live at twenty-eight Colmer Road, but they don't count because they'll be dead soon.'

'Robert, have you got a girlfriend?' I ask.

'I like Cleo at school, but she always puts her hand over her ears whenever anyone talks too loud.'

'Harry, do you like any of the girls at school?'

'No, they stink.'

'What about any of the film actresses? You like Jennifer Anniston, don't you?'

'Yeah, she's pretty, but I won't marry her because when I'm twenty-five, she'll be fifty-nine, so what's the point of getting together with an old broad?'

'So, you're never going to marry?'

'No, I don't want to grow up, I want to be with you and Mummy.'

'Mr McCarthy, this pizza is a bit burnt.'

'Yes. I'm sorry about that. I left it in the oven by mistake when I rushed out of the house.'

'You should've taken it out.'

'I didn't think about the pizza at the time, I was more concerned about you and Harry.'

'That's a bit weird, Mr McCarthy,' Robert says, as he carries on eating.

'These chips aren't that great either, but the lemonade tastes fine,' Robert adds.

I feel like I'm cooking a meal for Gordon Ramsey.

Robert is now focused on the two framed photos on the wall behind me.

'Those photos aren't in line with each other.'

I turn around and quickly glance at the photos of the McCarthy family and Harry.

'They look fine to me.'

'No, Harry's photo is half an inch lower than the other one. Were you going mad when you put them up?'

I get out of my chair and stand behind Robert to examine the photos again. They still look on the same level, so I go closer and I can now see that the family photo is fractionally higher.

'Oh yes, I see what you mean.'

'Are you going to change that today?'

'I'll leave it until tomorrow.'

'Don't forget, because this room looks stupid now.'

'I won't forget.'

I remember when Harry was about two, he used to meticulously line up all his DVDs on his bed, and he wouldn't allow me or Laura to touch them.

The rest of the meal is finished off without any further criticism of the pizza or the non-alignment of the photos.

A couple of hours later Stephanie arrives.

'Did you behave yourself for David?'

'Of course, but David shouted at us and told me to forget about Popeye.'

Stephanie looks up at me. 'Did he cause you any trouble?'

'Well, they did go to the sweet shop without telling me, while I was in the garden. It gave me a bit of a scare.'

'Robert's always doing that, I should've told you.'

Yes, you should have. 'That's OK.'

Stephanie collects the DVDs that Robert brought over and as they're walking out the front door, Robert turns around. 'Don't forget about those photos, Mr McCarthy.'

'I won't, thanks for reminding me.'

'Cheers, David,' Stephanie says.

'No problem, and good luck for tonight.'

Stephanie gives me a confident smile as if to say, 'don't worry about me, I've a game plan that cannot fail.'

It's only when the house is quiet again that I've the time to reflect on the events of this afternoon. This isn't the first time that Harry has run away. Whenever we go to a book or record shop Harry will nearly always attempt to wander off on his own, and on a handful of occasions he has succeeded. It's normally when

I'm looking at a book or CD. Sometimes it's easy to track him down, just go to where the *Thomas the Tank Engine* books section is, but two months ago he disappeared in HMV. I shouted his name several times, but he never responded. Even with the help of the security staff, it took an anxious five minutes before he was found, sitting on the floor with a few Ringo Starr CDs in his hand. Apart from playing drums in a disbanded pop group, Ringo also narrated the Thomas DVDs.

'Come on, Harry, we're going to see Mummy.'

'Oh all right, I'm going to bring my DVDs with me, because Mum has shit ones.'

'What did I say about the swearing?'

'The last time I was at Mum's, she watched a stupid film about a man singing and dancing outside his house, and it was raining. I've never seen anyone do that in Streatham.'

'Harry, that man is Gene Kelly, and he was one of the greatest dancers ever.'

'Yeah, right. How come I've never seen him on *Strictly*?'

'OK, get all your stuff together; we're leaving in a few minutes.'

Upon our arrival at Laura's, she gives Harry a warm hug, but he breaks away from her to venture into the living room, where he switches on the television.

'Do you want a cuppa?' Laura asks me.

'Robert came over this afternoon and the boys managed to get out of the house when I was in the garden,' I blurt out.

'They got out of the house?'

'Yes, but don't worry, I saw them running away and followed them in the car.'

I'm not in the habit of lying.

'How far did they get?'

'To the sweet shop.'

'But that's a good five-minute walk away.'

'I would've caught up with them sooner, but I couldn't find my car keys. Anyway I guessed where they were going.'

My lie is getting bigger by the minute.

'I can't believe it.'

'Laura, I'm sorry, I know it's my fault, but they didn't get too far.'

'Harry has to be accompanied wherever he goes, you know that.'

'It'll never happen again.'

Laura stares at the kitchen floor, and shakes her head.

'Haven't you ever made any mistakes?' I ask, rather too aggressively.

I know that Laura is angry, but to her credit she doesn't pursue the conversation.

'Let's change the subject,' Laura suggests.

There is a strained silence for a couple of minutes, before Laura speaks.

'Do you want to discuss the redundancy?'

'OK. I've got four weeks to go, I'm getting over twenty-eight grand and next week I'll start looking around for another job.'

'Twenty-eight thousand? You must be pleased with that?'

'I suppose so, but I'm worried about getting another job. My age is a big problem.'

I don't feel in the mood to discuss the redundancy, although I'm sure that Laura is.

'Laura, do you mind if Harry stays the night? I need some sleep,' I ask.

'Of course not, David. I'm sorry for losing my temper, but you can understand why I got upset?'

I'm pleased, if a little surprised, at Laura's sudden apology.

'I'd have reacted exactly the same,' I confess.

Laura leans forward and gives me a peck on the cheek, followed by a hug. I'm taken aback at the tenderness of that moment. It's like wiping out all those horrible arguments and turning the clock back to when we first met.

So much has happened in the past few years that I rarely reflect on the happier times that we once shared.

We met at a pub in Waterloo on Christmas Eve, nineteen ninety-eight. I was having a few drinks with my fellow postmen, when I noticed Laura at the bar. She looked stunning in a tight black skirt and red top. She was with her work colleagues. I mentioned how much I fancied Laura to my friend Alan, who promptly went over and told her. Laura came over to me and introduced herself. I found that we had a lot in common – a love of Italian food and sixties music, particularly The Beatles. We hit it off immediately and soon started seeing each other regularly. We were so carefree back then, that it now seems like I'm remembering someone else's life. We married on the sixth of July two thousand and two. I shall never forget how happy I felt on that day.

Perhaps that's one of the reasons I don't dwell on the past too much, because if I fast forward to today, it makes me sad.

'I'll pick Harry up at around eight o'clock tomorrow, is that OK?'

'Yes, that's fine. Harry, come here and say goodbye to your dad.'

Harry rushes out to the hallway.

'Daddy, why are you leaving? Is it because of Mum's cooking?'

'Harry, don't be so rude,' I sternly remind him

'Mummy, what's for dinner?'

'Jacket potato and chicken.'

'But jacket potatoes are for bald, mad people.'

I wonder if I fall into that category?

'Harry, give me a hug,' I say, arms outstretched.

'Make sure that you're not late tomorrow. There's a new episode of Thomas on ITV1 at ten past nine. I have to record it at home because Mum's cable never works properly.'

I attempt to embrace Harry, but he immediately pulls away. I manage to kiss the top of his head, before he dashes off.

'Thanks for taking care of Harry,' I say to Laura.

'Get a good night's sleep. You look tired.'

Our baby sitting network is non existent. My mother has never looked after Harry. Laura's parents were divorced when she was five. Her mother occasionally looked after Harry, when he was a baby, but she passed away a year before my Dad. Her father emigrated to Canada when Laura was ten. Her only contact with him is when she receives birthday and Christmas cards. He's never sent Harry a birthday card. I've suggested going on holiday to Canada and visiting her father, but she's not interested and rarely mentions him. Laura has an older sister called Amanda, who lives in Sheffield. Thankfully they are close and see each other quite regularly.

As I'm getting into my car, my mobile rings. It's Kerry.

'David, I'm going to ask a huge favour. Can you look after Niall tomorrow evening? Danny wants to see me alone.'

'I'm surprised you've asked me after yesterday, but of course I will. Why doesn't Danny want to see Niall?'

'The bastard says that there's a lot to discuss, and Niall will be a distraction.'

'I'm a little nervous about taking Niall out somewhere, so is it OK if I cook the boys a meal at home?'

'He'll love that, anything to do with food makes him happy. I am sorry for putting you in this position, but I need to know what Danny wants.'

Throughout the car journey home I can't stop thinking about Niall running across the road in Brighton. However, this is a different scenario. He'll be in the relative safety of my home and I'll have all the windows, front and back doors locked.

What can possibly go wrong?

Looking After Niall

At six o'clock the following morning I'm sitting in my garden smoking my first cigarette for five years. I'd bought a packet on the way home from Laura's. I resisted the temptation last night, but within a couple of minutes of waking up I unwrapped the packet with all the enthusiasm of a child tearing open his presents on Christmas morning.

With Harry staying at Laura's I should have used this opportunity to sleep longer, but years of interrupted sleep has meant that I require only a few hours of kip. Most retired people that I know are up at the crack of dawn every day because they've spent their working lives doing so. I'm about twenty-five years ahead of the game.

My thoughts quickly turn to my redundancy. I dread the thought of logging onto the Internet searching for computer programming jobs. Maybe a career change will be good for me, but where will I find a position that pays as much as I currently get?

As usual, any positive reaction is immediately followed by a negative one. I used to be more positive, but the stresses of the past few years have taken their toll. How can I not be affected by the pressure of bringing up Harry, virtually on my own?

Harry dominates my life. It seems like a lifetime ago when I used to regularly play tennis, go to the gym or meet my old friends for a drink. Now, I've no energy left to do anything other than work or look after my son.

In my darker moods I sometimes resent the way Harry has destroyed our marriage.

I remember how ecstatically happy we both were on the day we found out that Laura was pregnant. 'We're now a family,' she proudly announced.

Although it was a long labour – fourteen hours, there were no complications. However, during the next couple of years things slowly started to go wrong. His erratic sleeping patterns began to emerge and whilst you'd expect a newborn baby to only sleep a few hours a night you don't expect the same of a two-year-old. Little did we know that this was to continue for the next ten years and counting.

Laura often stayed up with Harry during this period. She said that I needed all my energy for my job.

This constant lack of sleep understandably made her edgy and the arguments, that were infrequent beforehand, were now almost daily.

Harry's odd behaviour also started to manifest, particularly his toiletry habits. He was still in nappies until he was nearly four. He frequently hid under the dining room table and smeared his excrement on chairs, the sofa, tables, dinner plates, his clothes, our clothes – you name it, he smeared it.

I read a book that teaches toilet training to severely handicapped children, so one Saturday I spent the whole day going through all the exercises in the book. This involved giving him lots of juices and running from the bedroom/living room/kitchen/garden to the toilet.

Every time he did a wee I'd give him a snack, usually crisps so that he would drink more. I also had various dolls to show how boys go to the toilet.

By four o'clock in the afternoon we were both exhausted. As I went into the kitchen to prepare the dinner, Harry did a number two in his nappy and smeared it on the television. I was so downhearted that I threw the book into the rubbish bin. However, the next day he successfully went to the toilet for the first time and has never soiled himself again.

Some days I feel sorry for myself and my situation, but I can't imagine what it must be like for Laura.

When I first met her, she was a happy and confident person. She had an excellent job, working for Barclays Bank and within a few months had been promoted to Accounts Manager. We had a lot of fun in those early years and engaged in our mutual interests: going to the theatre, cinema, museums, pubs and holidays abroad. Harry was born a year after our wedding. I had no doubts about Laura's abilities as a mother. She was, and still is, a caring and loving person and was looking forward to motherhood. The future looked good.

However, Harry's problems gradually began to affect Laura. She needed a break from looking after him, but unfortunately during this period I was working long hours and not always able to help her. She was prescribed anti-depressant tablets, but these made her lethargic and disinterested. On some weekends she wore only her dressing gown and rarely left the house.

When Harry was four years old Laura had a breakdown. She spent weeks in the hospital and when she came home she was irritable and sullen.

Our relationship reached breaking point shortly afterwards and when I told Laura that I wanted to leave, she simply nodded and asked if I could take Harry with me. Some of my friends question what sort of a mother would let their child go like that, but I always defend her. She was in no mental state to look after Harry, and it must have broken her heart to let him go. She has been trying to make up for it ever since.

Laura and me last lived together seven years ago, but only got divorced twelve months ago. We simply had too much to contend with on a daily basis to face a stressful divorce, or maybe subconsciously we thought that one day we'd get back together. Harry had to accompany us on the day of the divorce, as we couldn't get a baby-sitter. It was a welcome distraction on such a depressing day, even when he called my lawyer a 'boring, mad shit.'

The morning darkness has now been replaced by bright sunshine. I find this time of the day the most peaceful. God knows I've seen it enough.

Before breakfast I have another cigarette. Laura constantly nagged me about giving up smoking, so I'll need to get a packet of polos and hope that it disguises the smell. An hour and half and numerous polos later I arrive at Laura's.

'How is he?' I ask her.

'He's been OK. He was up at around five, but did sleep throughout the night. Coffee?'

'Yes, please.'

Harry rushes into the kitchen.

'It's time to split this joint,' he proclaims.

'Harry, shouldn't you give your Daddy a kiss?' Laura asks.

'Nah, can't be bothered.'

'Why don't you watch some telly? We'll be leaving soon,' I tell him.

Harry slowly walks out of the kitchen.

'We must stop him speaking to us like that,' Laura says.

'I know, but I'm not in the mood for a fight.'

'What are your plans today?' Laura diplomatically asks.

'We're seeing Mum.'

'Do you think she's ready for Harry? He upset her the last time.'

'She'll never be ready. I'm also looking after Niall tonight.'

'This is a wind up, right?'

'No, it isn't.'

'Have you gone mad? Forty-eight hours ago he tried to kill himself, remember?'

'That's not strictly true, but Kerry is meeting up with Danny to discuss their future. I couldn't say no.'

'Why are you always trying to impress Kerry?'

'Laura, don't be stupid, I'm simply helping her out. That's all.'

'And the fact that she's attractive and unattached has got nothing to do with this?'

'I don't need this right now, so can we drop it?' I demand, raising my voice.

'You seem down. Is it because of the redundancy?' Laura enquires.

'I've been thinking about everything in my life and it's made me depressed.'

'Once you start looking for a job, you'll feel better.'

'Are you sure about that? My life is shit. If I'm not working then I'm burdened with looking after Harry.'

'Burdened?'

'Yes, it's fucking hard work and I never get a break from it.'

'I help whenever I can.'

'I know, but it's not enough. I need a few weeks' or even months' break from him.'

'But that's impossible,' Laura says.

'No, it isn't. There's always residential schools.'

'We've been through this.'

'Things have changed. I'm getting older and he's getting bigger and stronger. I'm finding it increasingly harder to look after him.'

'I can let him stay here more often.'

'That's not the answer. He needs a structured environment. Look at how Mark has thrived since he's been at the Dorset school.'

Mark is a thirteen-year-old autistic boy that was in Harry's school. We regularly see his parents, Colin and Sue, who are always telling us how much he's progressed.

'But we'll never see him,' Laura pleads.

'We can have him back at weekends, as well as all the holidays. It'll be the best move for Harry.'

'Harry or you?' Laura asks.

'That's not fair.'

'You're pissed off about the redundancy and Harry will have to pay the consequences,' Laura shouts.

'You know that's not true. Didn't the school recommend residency for Harry a few months ago?'

'What the hell do they know? They have him during the day in a controlled environment. We deal with him in the real world,' Laura replies.

Laura pours the remainder of her coffee into the kitchen sink and looks ahead at the garden. All I can hear in the background is Ringo Starr's voice, telling us that Percy is a cross engine because Thomas bashed into his buffers.

'Laura, all I ask is that you think about it.'

Laura doesn't respond and continues to stare at the garden.

I walk into the living room, where Harry is still watching his Thomas DVD.

'Daddy, I want to get a Ringo Starr CD.'

'He used to play in a group called The Beatles, why don't I get you one of their CDs instead?'

'Nah, Ringo's music is much better than those morons.'

'Come on, Harry, gather your things up, it's time to go.'

A couple of minutes later he's rushing towards the front door.

'Harry, say goodbye to your mother.'

Harry reluctantly walks towards Laura, who hugs him tightly.

'I love you,' I hear her whisper to him.

'I'll speak to you soon,' I say to Laura, but she is already walking back to the kitchen.

'This isn't the way home,' Harry says, five minutes into the car journey.

'We're going to visit Grandma,' I explain.

'Why?'

'Because we haven't seen her in a couple of weeks.'

'But she never lets me squeeze her.'

'When you see Grandma you give her a gentle kiss, not a bear hug.'

'She always looks dead. Is she going to die today?'

'I hope not.'

Harry seems disappointed.

'Dad, are you married?'

'I was married to your mum, but we're now divorced, which means that we're not married anymore.'

Harry looks confused.

'Doesn't she like our house?'

'Yes, she does.'

'Then why does she live in that shithole?'

'It's not a shith… It's a nice flat.'

'Is she married?' Harry asks.

'No.'

'That means that you, Mummy, me and Figaro are not married.'

'Cats don't get married,' I say.

'Why not?'

'Harry, do you know what married means?'

'Yeah, men get out their willies.'

'Well not exactly, it means when a man and a woman love each other very much.'

'I love Thomas, can I marry Thomas?' Harry enquires.

'You cannot marry a train.'

'That's ridiculous,' Harry complains.

'Marriage is between a man and a woman. No cats or trains are involved.'

I think it's wise to avoid the gay marriages discussion for now.

My argument with Laura dominates my thoughts. I don't know why I suddenly blurted out about Harry going to a residential school. It's been on my mind for the past few months, but maybe Laura was right. Am I taking my frustrations out on Harry?

I've been feeling guilty about the school dilemma. I'll be admitting my failure as a parent if Harry ever had to go away. However, I'm convinced that he'll benefit enormously from it, although Laura doesn't agree and this makes it complicated.

Will I be physically able to look after Harry when I'm sixty? It'll break my heart to let Harry go and that's why I've put off this discussion for so long.

After visiting Mum I'll arrange to meet up with Colin and Sue, although I'm sure that Laura will dismiss this idea.

Fifteen minutes later we arrive at Mum's. She's waiting by the door as we walk up the driveway. Harry breaks free and runs towards Mum, who looks terrified.

'Harry, stop,' I shout, but he barges into Mum, knocking her over.

This isn't the best start to our visit.

'Jesus, Mary and Joseph,' I hear Mum mutter, as I pick her up.

'Mum, I'm sorry about that. Harry, what the hell do you think you're doing? You could have hurt Grandma.'

'Could?' Mum asks.

Harry merely shrugs his shoulders.

'Apologise now,' I demand.

'But she hasn't got a DVD player.'

'And neither will you if you don't apologise.'

'Oh, Grandma,' Harry says, with gritted teeth, as he squeezes her. I prise him away, but Mum now looks breathless.

'Say sorry to Grandma now,' I reiterate.

'David, don't worry about it. Any more apologies like that and I'm not going to see the day out,' Mum says.

Reluctantly I let it drop. Harry rushes upstairs to my old bedroom, while I follow my shaken mother into the kitchen.

'Mum, I'm sorry about that, he was too quick for me.'

'Does he do this to other people?' she asks.

'Sometimes.'

'Why does he dislike me so much?'

'He doesn't. He gets excited about coming here and that's the way he shows it,' I explain.

She sits down on the kitchen chair, still traumatised from her experience with Harry. Mum is seventy-two, but recently hasn't been in the best of health. Years of smoking has left a persistent cough and she's much thinner and weaker since my father passed away.

'Do you want a cuppa?' I ask.

Mum gratefully nods.

'How do they manage his behaviour at school?' Mum asks. 'Because he can't go around barging into people,' she adds.

'The school have various behavioural management classes for him and they say that he's doing well.'

'Do they? Well I haven't seen any improvement in him.'

That's typical Mum, always too honest. If I put on weight between visits she'll always tell me that I've got fat. In my mid twenties I was briefly engaged to Caroline. On one summer's evening Caroline broke up with me, and when I arrived home I dramatically threw her engagement ring across the living room, tearfully announcing our separation. 'Good job too,' was my mother's only response.

'So how's Laura?' Mum enquires.

'She's fine,' I say, handing Mum her cup of tea.

'Is she still taking those tablets?'

'No, she's off the anti-depressants now.'

'She's a mad woman altogether. No wonder Harry turned out the way he did.'

'Mum, let's not go through this again. Harry's problems are nothing to do with Laura.'

'Why don't you find yourself a nice, Irish girl?'

'I'm not interested in finding any women right now,' I defiantly respond.

'Well don't wait too long because in a couple of years no woman will have ya.'

Before I've time to ponder on my mother's kind words, Harry enters the kitchen.

'Can we go now?' he enquires.

'No, we've just got here,' I tell him.

Harry looks disappointed.

'Don't you like my house?' Mum asks.

'It sucks like you have no idea.'

'How many times must I tell you about being so rude?' I say to him.

'Harry, what job do you want to do when you get older?' Mum enquires, in a deliberate attempt to change the subject.

'I'm never going to work, that's for people who have hairs in their noses and ears.'

I'm hoping that Harry will hold down a job by the time he's twenty-one, even if it's stacking shelves at the local supermarket. A couple of months ago, whilst shopping there, I had a chat with the store manger, who told me that they hire special needs people, which was re-assuring to hear. Given Harry's problems I don't expect him to be a CEO at the Bank of England, but it wasn't that long ago when I thought that he'd never be employed. However, Harry's attitude will need to change. I can imagine him telling his manager to get lost if he was told to perform a task, which wouldn't be a good career move.

Mum gets up and hands Harry a photo of Dad.

'Do you remember Granddad?' she asks him.

'Yeah.'

'What do you remember about him?'

'His pimple above his left eyebrow.'

'Anything else?'

'He liked my Pokemon DVDs.'

'Yes, he was patient enough to sit through them with you.' Mum smiles, looking at me.

'Did he die because he didn't want to be with you any more?' Harry asks.

'No, he was very ill. We all die one day,' Mum solemnly replies.

'Dad and me think you're going to die today.'

'Have you got my funeral arranged already?' Mum asks me.

'Nothing to do with me, this is all Harry's work,' I tell her, holding my hands up.

'So when are you going to die?' Harry asks his grandma.

'Only the good Lord can answer that.'

'Who the hell is he?' Harry enquires.

'OK, Harry, why don't you play in the garden, but don't throw Grandma's chairs into the neighbour's garden.'

'But that's fun,' Harry protests, before dashing off.

We only spend another half-an-hour at Mum's. I hold Harry tightly when he kisses his Grandma goodbye and we leave without any further incidents. She looks relieved as we drive away. So do I.

A phone message is awaiting me back at the house.

'Is it OK to drop off Niall at three? Danny is taking me out for a meal and it'll take me a couple of hours to get ready.'

Why is Kerry bothering to make herself look presentable to a man that she loathes?

To minimise the risk of any further mishaps with Niall, I ask Laura if she would look after Harry again, and she readily agrees. An hour later I drop off a reluctant Harry at his mother's.

'This is the third time in eleven days that I have had to stay here, what's going on?' Harry asks me.

'I want to start looking for a new job and I have to do this on my own,' I lie, but I didn't want to let him know about Niall.

'I can't watch all my programmes here. Mum always watches that ridiculous *Coronation Street*.'

'Harry, that's her favourite programme.'

'But they all speak like aliens,' he complains.

Laura opens the front door and Harry slowly walks past her.

'He's a bit upset at you watching *Coronation Street*,' I say, smiling.

'The usual time in the morning?' Laura curtly enquires.

'Yeah, I'll be here at eight.'

She nods and swiftly closes the door. The residential school debate is still ongoing, albeit silently.

A few minutes after I get back to the house, Kerry and Niall arrive. I make her a coffee, while Niall ventures out to the garden.

'I'm sorry about Harry, but after what happened the other day I thought it's best to focus all my attention on Niall,' I tell Kerry.

'Of course I don't mind. I feel bad that I've messed up your day,' Kerry says, while sipping her coffee.

'Are you nervous about tonight?' I ask.

'A bit. I've no idea what his agenda is, but after eleven years of marriage he deserves a couple of hours of my time.'

Ten minutes later Kerry leaves, and soon afterwards I start cooking Niall's favourite meal – chips, sausage and beans.

As I look out of the kitchen I see that Niall is taking my clothes off the washing line.

'Stop that,' I shout as I rush towards him. However, once again he's too quick for me and manages to throw a handful of clothes into Mr Hennessy's garden, including a couple of pairs of my Y-fronts, which I'm sure Mr Hennessy will be less than delighted about retrieving.

I take the remaining clothes off the washing line and also pick up some of Harry's debris: a coat hanger, a Tony Bennett CD and the television remote control.

Niall immediately kicks the garden shed door, presumably as an act of protest. I head back to the kitchen to resume the meal, hoping that the dinner will settle him.

The smell of the sausages brings Niall back into the kitchen. He stands next to me and intently watches the sausages in the frying pan. He takes my hand and pushes it towards the pan, as if telling me that he wants to eat now.

'They're not ready yet.'

I expect a reaction, but he continues to stare at the sausages. I didn't realise that my cooking held such fascination.

After checking that the chips are not yet fully cooked, I close the oven door. Niall immediately stamps his foot and then gives me a mighty punch to my back. As I know only too well, Niall is a strong boy, so consequently my back is aching. A few seconds later he indiscriminately throws more punches at me and hits me on my testicles.

I collapse to the floor, unable to catch my breath. Niall merely glances at me before opening the oven door. I can only look on as he takes out the tray of chips, before reacting against the heat, causing the tray to fall onto the floor. Any pain he may be suffering is forgotten, as he sits down amongst the chips and starts to eat them.

'Niall, no,' I mutter, but he ignores me and continues with his impromptu dinner.

I stagger to my feet and usher him out to the garden, where he sadly peers at the remaining chips through the kitchen window. It takes several more minutes to fully catch my breath, when I throw away the nearly cooked chips and put a fresh load in the oven. Niall notices this and head-butts the window in protest.

I approach him.

'The dinner won't be ready for another twenty minutes,' I say.

He stares at me, looking confused. I wish that I knew more Makaton symbols so that I can communicate better, for as frustrated as I am, it must be a million times worse for him.

I need to keep him occupied, but as he shows little interest in anything other than food, this will be difficult. However, I bring him into the living room and put on a Thomas DVD. He watches it for only a few seconds before walking back into the kitchen, where he sits at the dining table, staring at the oven.

'Good waiting,' I tell him, glad that for the time being he's settled, which is more than can be said for my testicles, which feel like they will explode. This isn't a new experience for me, Harry was five the last time this happened. We were walking across Clapham High Street when, for no apparent reason, he smacked me where it hurts the most. Naturally I collapsed in the middle of the road, breathless and unable to move. Two cars came to a screeching halt, narrowly missing me.

Niall remains seated for the next half an hour and as I hand him his plate he flaps his arms in excitement. This isn't a usual reaction to my cooking. When Harry first moved in with me Laura suggested that I should attend cookery classes as a matter of urgency.

He smells the first half a dozen chips before eating them, but quickly scoffs down the rest of his meal. He then rests his fork on my plate, indicating that he wants some of my dinner, so I simply hand him my plate. I can do with losing some weight anyway.

After the meal I join Niall in the garden.

'Did you enjoy the dinner?' I ask.

Niall stares ahead, without any acknowledgment.

'Would you like some dessert?'

Niall turns to look at me, pressing his four fingers to his chin. This is a Makaton symbol for food. I'm pleased that he's understood me, but I wonder if he deliberately ignored me beforehand?

After gobbling down two helpings of ice cream, with chocolate topping, Niall returns to the garden. I'm sitting near him, drinking a can of Coke. Every few minutes he takes a gulp of my drink. Food and drink don't have any personal boundaries as far as Harry and Niall are concerned.

When normal children visit our house they always explore the toys, books and DVDs in Harry's room, but Niall has no such interest. He simply potters around the garden. When something excites him he makes loud, grunting noises and flicks his fingers in front of his face.

It's been two hours since Kerry left and apart from a bruised back and testicles that have doubled in size, the afternoon has gone better than I expected. Kerry will probably be back in two to three hours, so I'm nearly halfway there. I immediately feel guilty, thinking that looking after Niall is a chore. He deserves better.

I find one of Harry's Action Men and hand it to Niall. He gives it straight back to me, indicating that he wants the clothes removed, which I do and Niall happily takes it off me. Within a couple of minutes the Action Man is beheaded.

Niall's grunting noises get louder as he pulls and prods his new toy. Occasionally he stops doing this, to stare blankly ahead of him.

'What are you thinking about?' I ask.

He makes no acknowledgement and the blank stare continues. I wonder what's it like inside his trapped mind?

Every so often he lies down and rests his cheek on the patio, then turns over and does the same with the other cheek. He repeats this on all the windows and the garden panels. I guess this is all to do with his heightened sensory awareness.

He then walks slowly towards me, but stumbles. He reaches for me, but collapses at my feet. His head and body start violently shaking. As we're on the patio his head hits the concrete several times before I can put my hand around it. Although I've never seen an epileptic fit I'm certain that Niall is having one.

With my spare hand I manage to dial 999 on my mobile and someone immediately answers.

'A twelve-year-old boy is having a fit, what the fuck shall I do?' I shout.

'Turn him on his side so that he doesn't swallow his tongue and protect his head from bashing against the floor,' she says.

I manage to turn him on his side.

'How long has he been having the fit?' she asks.

'I don't know, maybe a couple of minutes. Why?'

'They usually last three to four minutes.'

Tears are rolling down my face as I look at poor, helpless Niall. Then, at last the shaking stops and he lays still as if in a deep sleep. His face is deathly pale, but it seems that he's breathing normally.

'He's stopped shaking, but he looks awful. Please get an ambulance here now,' I yell.

After giving the operator my address, I then explain Niall's autism. I hear her pass on this information and she reassuringly talks to me until the ambulance arrives.

The paramedics immediately introduce themselves as Geoff and Andrea.

Niall is still sleeping when Geoff checks his pulse. He uses some device to pinch the top of one of Niall's fingers. Niall flinches when he does this.

'That's a good sign,' he tells me.

Geoff then puts an oxygen mask over Niall's face, which he doesn't react to.

'It looks like he's had a grand mall seizure. Has he had one before?' Geoff asks me.

'I don't know. I need to contact his mother.'

'He should be OK, but we need to take him to the hospital for further tests.'

'Why isn't he coming around?' I ask.

'It takes a while to recover; he should be conscious within an hour, but he'll be lethargic for days.'

Geoff and Andrea gently move Niall into the ambulance and I accompany them.

I look at Niall with the mask covering his innocent and beautiful face. Why isn't there any justice in this world? Doesn't he have enough to deal with already? Once again tears roll down my face. The ambulance lady looks at me, but doesn't say anything. She probably sees this reaction many times during her working day.

As we're approaching the hospital Niall starts to come around. He immediately takes the mask off and looks around at his unfamiliar surroundings.

'Niall, you've had an accident and we're taking you to the hospital, but don't worry, you're going to be OK,' I tell him.

It must be difficult enough explaining to a normal child that they have just had an epileptic fit, but how do you begin to tell a severely autistic child, who has no language?

Every time Andrea attempts to put his mask back on, Niall immediately removes it. She eventually gives up. He then sits up and rushes to open the door, but we pull him away.

'Niall, the doctors have to do some tests on you,' I say to him.

He grits his teeth and bangs his head with his fist. Andrea immediately stops him, as she's probably worried that this might trigger another fit.

Two nurses and a doctor meet us when we arrive at the hospital and within a few minutes the doctor attempts to examine Niall, but he doesn't co-operate.

'We need to do an ECG, but with special needs children we normally give a sedative powder, which we will administer through his nose.'

'Good luck with that,' I say.

'I'll get half a dozen staff to hold him down. I know that this is unpleasant, but it's the only way. I need to monitor his heart. I understand you're not his father?' the doctor asks.

'No, I was babysitting for his mum.'

'We need her permission before we can do this.'

'I haven't had the chance to contact her yet. Can someone look after Niall so I can ring her?'

The doctor brings over two nurses, while I step outside the hospital and dial Kerry's mobile.

'Kerry, it's David.'

'Hi, David, how's it going with Niall?'

'Bad news I'm afraid. He had an epileptic fit about an hour ago and we're at Croydon University hospital,' I blurt out, but there's no room for small talk.

'Oh my God, is he OK?'

'He's confused and scared. They want to do an ECG, but need your go-ahead.'

'Please tell them to do it. I'll be there in twenty minutes.'

'They keep asking me whether he's had a fit before?'

'No, he hasn't. I can't believe this. Let me go.'

She hangs up.

Half an hour later I'm sitting in a room full of doctors and nurses. Niall is wandering around the room, making his usual grunting noises. He has made a couple of dashes for the door, but even Niall can't get pass the two burly male nurses. Then Kerry bursts in and rushes to her son.

'Oh, my boy, how are you?' Kerry says, as she hugs him tightly. He looks over her shoulder to see if she has left an escape route.

Kerry cannot stop crying and won't let go of Niall. The doctor tells Kerry that he needs to do an ECG as soon as possible and explains what's about to happen. Within a few minutes seven of us are holding him down on the bed like a caged animal while the doctor gives him the required sedative. Kerry holds his hand and constantly reassures him.

A short time later Niall is asleep and the doctors and nurses go about their job. I step outside the room and grab a cup of coffee down the corridor. It isn't long before Kerry joins me.

'They tell me that the first few readings look fine, but need to get a more detailed picture. They want him to stay here overnight in case he has another fit. I'll stay with him,' Kerry says.

'At least that's good news about the tests,' I say.

'What happened?' Kerry asks.

Her eyes, red from crying, stare at the floor.

I explain the last hour and a half to her. She shakes her head in disbelief, but doesn't respond.

'There's a connection between autism and epilepsy. Several children in Harry's class have epilepsy,' I explain to her.

'And that's supposed to make me feel better?'

There's a strained silence between us for a couple of minutes.

'I'm sorry, I didn't mean that.'

'Don't worry,' I tell her, holding my hand up.

'Have they talked about medication yet?' I ask.

'He'll have to take eight tablets a day of some drug called Epilim. As he won't swallow tablets I'll have to crush them up and somehow mix them in with his cereal and dinner. That'll be fun,' she replies, still looking at the floor.

'I don't know how I'm going to cope.'

'You have to be strong. Niall needs you.'

'And who's going to look after me?'

'Things didn't go well with Danny?' I enquire.

'The shit told me that he still loves me, but will only come back if Niall is taken into care. Of course he dressed it up, making it sound that it was the best move for Niall, but he's only thinking of himself.'

This subject matter is a hot potato of late.

'I presume his lady friend is no longer around?'

'The trollop left him last week. At least she had the sense not to waste years on that bastard,' Kerry says, raising her voice.

Half an hour passes, mostly in silence. I'm finding it difficult to find the right words to comfort her.

'I better get back to Niall. He'll be waking up shortly.'

'I hope you both get a good night's sleep. I'll ring you tomorrow.'

'David, thanks so much for reacting calmly to every-thing, I'd have gone to pieces. I owe you a few babysit-ting sessions, and so much more.'

'Please give Niall a kiss for me. I can't tell you how much it hurt me to see him like that.'

We hug each other tightly and I watch her disappear into Niall's ward.

As soon as I leave the hospital I ring Laura.

'I'm picking up Harry in ten minutes, is that OK?' I ask.

'He can stay here, it's no problem,' Laura says.

'Thanks, but I need him with me tonight.'

Doctor Wilkes

At four-fifteen the following morning I'm sitting with Harry in the living room. Harry has been awake for the last hour.

Although most of the time I can get by with the minimum required sleep, sometimes it does catch up on me. I recently had a meeting at work with a client that I'd never met before. Whilst he was talking to me I kept dozing off. Although the subject matter was extremely boring, this wasn't my most impressive career move.

We're watching a Pokemon DVD. I've sat through hundreds of hours watching Harry's favourite programmes, but Pokemon totally baffles me. But that's probably down to me, as the rest of the world absolutely loves it.

However, the popularity of Pokemon was waning by the time Harry latched onto it. I clearly remember having the cinema to ourselves one afternoon, when Harry and I went to see one of the later Pokemon films. As usual I found the film was as incomprehensible as its predecessors and by the time the end-of-film credits appeared my mental state was so fragile that I stood up and applauded, while continuously shouting 'bravo'. I'm not sure what the projectionist made of that.

I still feel shaken by yesterday's events. It's the first time that I've witnessed an epileptic fit. Niall's illness and Danny's conditional reconciliation proposal didn't make it a good day for Kerry. Danny gave her a choice – either him or Niall. I hope that she told Danny where he can stick his ultimatum.

I know only too well the pain of a marriage break-up. However, I've been lucky in having a supportive partner.

While looking after Harry is a daily struggle, it's much harder for Kerry. Niall's illness will only increase her stress levels.

Although I was only given custody of Harry one year ago, I've been living alone with my son for the past seven years. There have been many times when I've felt at breaking point. When Laura was very ill she saw little of Harry, which didn't seem to concern him much. Taking the sole responsibility for my son was hard to adjust to initially. I started work late because I had to drop Harry off at school and finished early as I had to pick him up from school. I tried to make up the time by home working, but this proved impossible when Harry was also in the house, as he needed full time care and attention.

It was two years after Laura's breakdown when she felt able to look after Harry overnight. I was really looking forward to that first night of freedom and arranged to meet a group of friends at a local pub. However I left after an hour as I desperately missed my son and wanted to speak with him.

'Tell Mummy to get rid of the three red cars on her street, they look ridiculous,' he told me.

I tried to explain that these cars didn't belong to Mum, but he wasn't interested in the small print.

I went to bed on my own that night for the first time in years; it was a strange experience.

Laura told me that he had little sleep that night as he kept looking at the red cars from his bedroom window.

'There're showing the last Harry Potter film at the Odeon again. Do you wanna see it?' I ask Harry.

'But Harry Potter's voice has changed.'

'What do you mean?'

'In the *Philosopher's Stone* his voice was different.'

'That's because he was a boy then. As you get older your voice changes.'

'Daniel Ratcliffe lives in London. Can we go to his house?'

'I don't know where he lives.'

'The guard at Victoria station will know.'

'No, he won't. Now do you want to see the film?'

'Nah, his voice is crap now.'

Two hours later we're sitting in the doctor's reception room. This is my yearly check up. Harry is reading the *Hello* magazine.

'Oh look, it's Alec Baldwin,' Harry excitedly says.

I look at the article recalling the messy divorce between Alec Baldwin and Kim Basinger.

'How do you know about him?' I ask.

'He plays Mr Conductor in *Thomas and the Magic RailRoad*.'

I should have guessed.

'But it doesn't say anything about Thomas,' Harry disappointedly adds.

'Harry, the article is all about his divorce from his wife a few years ago. Remember when we talked about divorce?'

Harry stares blankly at me.

'That's when a man and a woman no longer live together,' I explain.

'But can that be? Baldwin is a genius.'

The doctor conveniently calls us in.

'This is my son, Harry,' I say, as we enter the doctor's office.

'Who the hell are you?' Harry enquires.

'Don't be so rude,' I tell my son.

'I'm Doctor Wilkes. I'm going to examine your dad.'

'Why are all those hairs coming out of your nose?' Harry asks the doctor.

'Harry, please be quiet,' I reiterate. Harry seems obsessed with hairy noses.

'David, that's OK. My wife is always onto me about that,' the doctor smiles at Harry.

'Doctors are shit. They always let people die.'

'Some people are so ill, that even the doctor cannot help them,' the doctor patiently explains.

'If I jumped off a very high building, would I die?'

'Probably.'

'Then you're shit as well.'

'Harry, that's enough of this. If you talk anymore we're not going to Burger King.'

Harry stays quiet for the time being.

After a number of questions the doctor tells me that I need to lose two stone, drink less and exercise more. Nothing earth shattering there. However, he looks concerned after taking my blood pressure.

'One hundred and forty-two over ninety, that's too high. Do you have a history of high blood pressure in the family?'

'Not that I'm aware of,' I say.

He takes my blood pressure again and this time it's one hundred and forty-five over ninety-three This is probably due to the increased stress levels after the last reading. It's having a snowball affect.

'What's your job?' the doctor asks.

'I'm a computer programmer, but I've just been made redundant.'

'This could be stress-related. The loss of your job, plus bringing up an autistic boy on your own are contributing factors.'

'Hopefully I'll find another job, but Harry's situation is never going to change,' I respond.

'I know and I sympathise, but as you get older it's going to be increasingly difficult for you. Does he get any respite?'

'Not much.'

'I'll write a letter to Social Services, stressing the need for respite, not only for Harry's needs, but also to help you.'

The doctor immediately writes a prescription for blood pressure tablets and hands it to me.

'How long do I need to take these for?' I ask.

'Indefinitely. Come back and see me in two months and we'll review it then. In the meantime try to do some exercise, it's the best stress reliever.'

Harry approaches the doctor, takes a piece of fluff from his jacket and puts it in the bin. He stands in front of the doctor looking intently at his jacket.

'Where did that fluff come from?' he asks the doctor.

'I'm not sure.'

'Daddy, I don't trust him. He wears dirty jackets and is evil.'

'Harry, this doctor is not evil and everyone has fluff on their clothes.'

'I don't and neither do you.'

'Doctor, we'd better go. I'm sorry about Harry's behaviour.'

'There's no need to be. It's not everyday that I'm told that I'm evil, shit at my job, have overgrown hairs up my nose, and wear a dirty jacket. Wait a minute I haven't seen my wife yet.' The doctor smiles.

A doctor with a sense of humour? Well I never.

Harry continues to stare suspiciously at Doctor Wilkes as we leave his office.

How can this be possible? Everything was OK when I had my regular check-up last year, and I was under more stress then, as the divorce proceedings were drawing to a close.

I wish I'd asked the doctor more questions. I assume the risk of having a heart attack has now increased? Somehow I have to control the stress levels in my life, but with Harry that's going to be difficult.

Will this affect getting another job? I would have to put this on the medical history form.

'Daddy, I want to go to Burger King,' Harry tells me, as we get into the car.

'Fuck you,' I shout back.

'What about McDonalds then?'

'My life is a mess and all you're concerned about is stuffing a burger down your throat,' I yell at Harry.

'So where are we going then?' Harry calmly enquires.

I close my eyes and shake my head in despair. I regret my outburst. I'm blaming him for things that are wrong in my life. How can I condemn someone that is born into autism?

Am I over dramatising everything? Lots of people have high blood pressure and lead normal lives. I must start exercising and stop using Harry as an excuse for not doing so.

'Why isn't the old *Batman* TV series on the telly anymore?' Harry asks.

Fuck knows is my immediate thought, but I hold off a few seconds before replying.

'I'm not sure.'

'Adam West is brilliant. He was born in Washington, in America, on the nineteenth of September in nineteen twenty-eight. He was in one hundred and twenty episodes of *Batman* between nineteen sixty-six and nineteen sixty-eight. Why doesn't he play Batman again?'

'He may be too old to be climbing up buildings.'

Harry looks confused.

'Some days you just can't get rid of a bomb,' he states.

At least this remark brings a wry smile to my face. In the nineteen sixties' *Batman* film there is a scene where Batman is running along a sea front trying to safely throw away a bomb, which is a black ball with a fuse at the end of it. With every attempt to dispose of it someone suddenly appears – a couple of nuns, the Salvation Army, a mother with a child and even some ducks. It's at this point when he turns to the camera and recites the immortal 'can't get rid of a bomb' sentence. This reminds me when Harry and I went into the London Underground the day after the terrorist attack. All the TV cameras were out in force and they must have thought how brave we were. Harry was going through a London Underground phase, where we'd ride the Victoria, Central and Piccadilly lines all day, only leaving when it was time to go home. He had watched the Batman film that morning and throughout the whole day kept saying 'some days you just can't get rid of a bomb.' Needless to say we got some nervous looks.

'I want Batman to kick that shithead doctor up his fat arse.'

'OK, Harry, let's forget about Batman and the doctor for now.'

'It's eleven minutes past two. I'll have to eat my burger in twenty-two minutes,' Harry announces, as we leave the doctor's office.

'Why?'

'We're going to Bernadette's house.'

'The girl in your class?'

'Yes, her name is Bernadette O'Leary, she was born on the sixteenth of March two thousand and three at ten thirty-six in the morning. Her mother's name is Alice, she's thirty-nine and smells of shit perfume. Her dad is Francis, he's forty-one and his eyes are too wide.'

'Thanks for the update, but did you invite yourself around to their house?'

'Yes, Bernadette told me to come around at three o'clock.'

Inviting himself around to another person's house is a regular occurrence for Harry, but visiting a girlfriend is a first.

'Is Bernadette your new friend?' I ask, deliberately leaving out the word girl.

'She's my fifth best friend.'

So she's jumped into the top five. Harry has never shown a romantic interest before and this is unlikely to lead that way too, but the thought that he could develop a relationship with Bernadette fills me with hope.

'Does Alice know that you're coming around?'

Harry shrugs his shoulders. 'Don't know, don't care.'

'Never mind, we'll find out soon enough.'

Fifteen minutes later we're having our lunch at Burger King.

'Harry, I'm sorry for losing my temper with you earlier.'

'What do you mean?'

'I shouldn't have sworn at you.'

'But swearing is beautiful. Daddy, why doesn't Thomas ever say fuck or shit?'

'Because Thomas knows that they are rude words.'

I can't believe that I'm using Thomas as a role model.

'I could teach Thomas swear words and he can call Percy a fat, bollocks bastard.'

'Eat your burger, we've got to leave shortly.'

My original attempt at an apology has ended up as a swearing exercise for Harry.

'Daddy, why did you go to the toilet in Burger King? We're two minutes late now,' Harry asks, as we are walking up the driveway to Bernadette's house.

'Sorry, but I had to go.'

Harry simply shakes his head.

Alice answers the door.

'Hi, come in,' she says.

'Have you got any Frosties?' Harry enquires, before entering the house.

'Harry, instead of being so rude, why don't you say hello to Alice?'

'Yeah hi, well have you?' Harry stretches out the palm of hands as if she will immediately give him a handful of Frosties.

'Yes, we have. Do you want some?'

'Well of course.'

'Harry can be a bit full on,' I say.

'Don't worry, I understand,' Alice replies, as we walk into the kitchen.

Alice is a pretty woman. She's immaculately dressed, in a blue skirt and white top.

'I'm sorry about the mess, but Bernadette only told me a few minutes ago that you were coming.'

I glance around the kitchen; it looks perfect.

Bernadette rushes into the kitchen. She's a small child, with long blonde hair and blue eyes. She looks like her mother.

'What's your name?' she asks.

'David.'

'Why is it David?'

'I'm not sure. My parents called me that.'

'Why the hell did they do that?'

'I don't know, but I shall ask,' I tell her.

'Harry told me that you are always saying fuck.'

'Well, I wouldn't say that I always use that word, but sometimes it slips out,' I try to explain.

'Harry told me that you called your neighbour a fucking arsehole and your boss a fucking prick, and a footballer a ...'

'OK, Bernadette, why don't you tell Harry that his Frosties are ready?' Alice interrupts.

'I was wondering where my daughter picked up those vulgar words. Mystery solved.'

I can think of no adequate response.

'Coffee?' she asks.

'No, I'm fine, thanks,' trying not to sound too eager to leave.

'Harry will come down in a couple of minutes, he's just having a shit,' Bernadette casually remarks.

Alice closes her eyes, but doesn't respond.

'Do you like United Airlines?' Bernadette asks.

'They're OK.'

'OK?'

Bernadette looks puzzled.

'You're joking, right?' she enquires.

Now I'm confused.

'One airline is much the same as the next,' I try to explain.

'United Airlines are the dog's bollocks.'

'Bernadette, what did I say about swearing?' her mother interrupts.

'Did you enjoy the UA9752 flight that you took on the twenty-fifth of July two thousand and thirteen?' Bernadette asks

'I can't remember.'

'Harry told me that your plane to Orlando, Florida, United States Of America, left Heathrow Airport at eight twenty-six in the morning and you arrived in Orlando at twelve forty-one American time. There are three different time zones in the United States Of America and Florida is five hours behind Streatham time. It was ninety-one degrees when you landed and Harry's bollocks were dripping of sweat.'

I've no answer to that.

'The number of the return flight was UA9753 and you arrived at Heathrow at eight fifty-three on August fourth. On July the twenty-sixth, twenty-seventh, twenty-ninth and August the second you went to Disney World. Did you meet Buzz Lightyear?'

'I don't think so.'

'I want him to autograph the sole of my shoe. If I give you my shoe, will you get his autograph when you next go to Disney World?'

'It's best to clear that with your mum first.'

I can't remember too much about the flight, but I do recall our holiday. Like most children, Harry was keen to visit Disney World. However the combination of the heat and the length of time queuing up for the rides proved too much for him. Laura and I got the brunt of his punches, kicks and head-butts, but whoever was in the firing line also suffered, which resulted in several confrontations. 'You shouldn't have put him in this situation', 'he doesn't belong here' and 'can't you control him better?' were a few remarks that I can still remember.

One elderly American man called me 'a limey asshole', but did apologise when I explained Harry's autism.

As this was my idea to visit Disney World, Laura made it abundantly clear that it was too ambitious to make such a trip.

All in all it was a stressful holiday.

'United Airlines have a twelve point Customer Commitment plan that is amazing. Number one is to advise about lowest available fares, two: notify customers of known delays, cancellations and diversions.'

Alice walks over to the kitchen sink to continue the washing up. She's obviously heard this plan before.

'Three: deliver baggage on time, four: allow reservations to be canceled for a certain period after purchase, five: provide prompt ticket refunds, six: properly accommodate passengers with disabilities and other special needs, seven: meet customers' essential needs during lengthy tarmac delays, eight: treat passengers fairly and consistently in the case of oversales.'

I'm beginning to lose the will to live.

'Nine: disclose travel itinerary, cancellation policies, frequent flyer rules and aircraft configuration, ten: notify customers about travel itinerary changes in a timely manner.'

I look over at Alice to attempt to get her attention, so that I can get out of this situation, but she's obviously tuned out of this one-way conversation.

'Eleven: ensure responsiveness to customer complaints and number twelve: provide service to mitigate inconveniences resulting from cancellations and misconnections.'

'That's impressive,' I say.

'Do you want to hear the British Airways commitment plan?'

'No, thanks,' I reply, a little too quickly.

'Virgin?'

'Can you leave David alone now, Bernadette?'

I was beginning to wonder whether Bernadette's mother did actually exist.

Harry enters the kitchen and Bernadette approaches him.

'Harry, please open your mouth,' she asks and Harry duly obliges.

She puts her nose inside his mouth and sniffs.

'You used Colgate Plus 100 this morning,' she confidently exclaims.

'Right on the button, sister,' Harry excitedly replies, as they give each other a high five.

I've never seen Harry interact in such a way before, and the moment immediately affects me.

'Can I use your toilet?' I ask Alice.

'Of course, it's up the stairs and first on your left.'

A few tears flow down my cheeks. To most normal parents the high-five interaction would mean nothing, but for Harry to respond in such an appropriate manner is a giant leap forward.

I wipe the tears away and attempt to compose myself before returning to the kitchen. Three pairs of eyes greet me.

'Your eyes are full of water,' Harry says.

'It's only hay fever.'

'What the hell is that?'

'It means that you are allergic to plants and flowers.'

'I've never seen any flowers in Streatham, it's a shithole.'

'Did you know that George Carlin died on the twenty-second of June two thousand and eight?' Bernadette asks.

'He was the Thomas narrator, right?'

'He was in the American Thomas series from nine-teen ninety-one to nineteen ninety-eight. He had grey hair on his face but no hair on his head; that's a bit weird.'

Before I have a chance to respond Bernadette continues.

'George Carlin loved Thomas, do you love Thomas?'

'He's OK,' is my compromise response.

'Do you want to see my Thomas DVD and book col-lection?' Bernadette asks, as if encouraged by my response.

Just as I'm thinking about my get out clause, Bernadette continues.

'My dad told me on September the twenty-third two thousand and nine that Thomas should be used for scrap metal. What's scrap metal?'

'David has to go now,' Alice tells her daughter.

'My dad always smells of ladies' perfume, but it's not the same perfume as Mummy's.'

Alice looks away from her daughter. This moment has immediately entered the top ten most embarrassing experiences of my life and there have been many. Some are ongoing; Harry helping himself to stranger's meals or drinks in restaurants and pubs, whereas some are thankfully one-offs – kissing an extremely fat woman on the backside while waiting in a Post Office queue is one that I, and she, will never forget.

'I'd love to look at your Thomas DVDs and books,' I say to Bernadette, breaking through the silence.

Love is a bit strong. Hate would have been more appropriate, but Bernadette's expression, when she asked me, was willing me to say yes. I'm also sympathetic to her needs, as it seems that all is not well in the O'Leary household.

'David, you don't have to,' Alice reassures me.

'It's OK. Can I have that coffee now please?'

Alice nods, probably relieved that I didn't ask her who owns the perfume that her husband smells of.

I'm feeling slightly deranged after been told the life story of Thomas for the past hour, but I hide my feelings well as I prepare to leave.

'I don't like your grey eyebrows, why are they like that?' Bernadette asks, standing only a few inches away from me.

Before I have the chance to reply she grabs my left eyebrow and with amazing strength removes a handful of hairs. The pain is excruciating.

'That's better,' Bernadette delightedly says, as she examines the grey hairs in her hand.

'What the fu …' I stop just in time.

'Bernadette, that was a terrible thing to do. Go upstairs now,' Alice shouts at her daughter.

'But *Scooby Do* isn't on telly tonight,' Bernadette objects, as she stares menacingly at my right eyebrow.

'If you don't go now, I'm going to tell Daddy what happened.'

'But he has grey eyebrows as well.'

'Don't you mean he *used* to have them? Now go and play with Harry.'

Bernadette reluctantly leaves.

I look at the kitchen mirror and notice that there's a bald patch where my left eyebrow used to be. I look like a simpleton.

'I'm sorry about that,' Alice says.

'No worries. I've had worse.'

I'm trying hard to think what. Niall's punch to my testicles probably beats it, which is little consolation.

Moments later Harry comes bounding into the kitchen.

'I like your toilet paper, Mrs O'Leary,' Harry says, as Alice hands him another bowl of Frosties.

'Do you want milk this time?' she asks.

'Get the fuck out of here,' Harry snaps.

'Harry, that's enough. One more swear word and you're going home.'

'But milk is ghastly.'

I can't help but smile, much to Alice's displeasure. I've never heard him say ghastly before. I'm pleased that at least he appears to have understood my warning about swearing.

Harry eagerly delves into his milk-free Frosties.

'Is it OK if I pop back at six?' I ask.

'That's fine.'

As I walk into the hallway Bernadette jumps from the stairs in front of me. I immediately step back, fearing another eyebrow attack.

'I have to shut the door quietly,' Bernadette remarks.

'She has a thing about noise,' Alice explains.

For the first time I see a gentle smile on Alice's face. I sometimes forget the stresses that other parents of autistic children go through.

After spending the next two hours researching everything you wanted to know about high blood pressure but were afraid to ask, I'm in a thoroughly depressed state of mind. The messages are clear – reduce stress, weight and alcoholic intake and increase exercise. Doctor Wilkes, you're a genius, despite what Harry said. I also looked at a number of job positions that matched my skill set, all of which paying considerably lower than I am currently earning.

Thankfully the sound of my phone ringing interrupts my thoughts.

'David, it's Kerry. Are you in this afternoon?'

'Yeah, I'm picking up Harry soon and we're heading straight back here. Why?'

'There's been a development with Danny; can I pop around?'

Actually I'm wallowing in self-pity right now, so it's not convenient.

'No problem.'

'I hate to impose, but I'll be eternally grateful if I could stay tonight,' Kerry tells me, as she walks up my driveway, pulling a travel case.

Over a cup of coffee she explains that Danny refuses to accept that their marriage is over and is coming to her house tonight to discuss it further.

'Isn't that a positive sign?' I ask.

'It's going to turn into a massive argument, and I don't feel up to it right now. I could've stayed with my mum or sister, but when he discovers that we're not home he'll visit both of them. They don't know that I'm here. As he's not aware of our friendship, he wouldn't think of coming here.'

This is the last thing that I need right now.

'Glad that I can help.'

I look out to the garden where Niall is sitting amongst the rose bushes, eating the few remaining petals, but not before putting salt on them.

'Niall has got hold of the salt container,' I tell Kerry.

She rushes out to the garden, but before she reaches Niall he throws the salt container into our neighbour's garden. A defeated Kerry returns to the kitchen.

'I'm sorry about that. I can climb over the fence to get it back.'

'Don't worry, it'll be returned soon enough. I need to cut down on my salt intake anyway.'

I don't bother to explain my recent health problems.

'Does Niall want to watch a DVD?'

'No thanks. He has no interest in TV.'

'I can make him chips and sausages. He seemed to enjoy that the last time.'

Kerry smiled and nodded. A few minutes later the smell of food brings Niall into the kitchen. He sits on the kitchen floor, intensely studying the oven.

Soon afterwards Harry comes rushing into the kitchen and opens the oven door.

'My favourite meal. This is beautiful and bollocks food. My belly is going to get bigger.'

Niall ignores Harry's presence, but stands up to get a closer look inside the oven, while it is open. He looks admiringly at the chips and sausage, as if this was the first time that he's seen such an amazing meal.

'Do you think that Harry has tourette's?' Kerry asks.

'No, he has a mild form of ADHD.'

'Is that Attention Deficient Disorder?'

'Yeah, with hyperactivity thrown in.'

'Oh, I wasn't aware he had that,' Kerry responds.

'Our paediatrician diagnosed ADHD when he was four. He's been on Ritalin since then.'

'Has it helped?'

'Considerably. He couldn't concentrate on anything and was always getting into fights at school, usually instigated by himself. Since he's been taking Ritalin he's been calmer and able to focus better at school.'

'Sorry, I didn't know.'

'I usually tell people he's autistic, but don't mention the ADHD; it's much easier.'

'Life can be shit, don't you think?' Kerry aggressively states.

The doorbell interrupts our conversation.

'Hi, can I come in?' Laura asks.

'Of course. I wasn't expecting you.'

'I wanted to find out how you got on at the doctor's,' Laura explains, before noticing the travel case in the hallway.

'Have you got visitors?' she asks.

'Kerry is staying overnight.'

'It certainly looks like this relationship has moved on since our last conversation.'

'Laura, for the last time, there's nothing going on between us, OK?' I say, a little too loudly. 'She's having problems with Danny and couldn't face another confrontation with him.'

'It's none of my business anyway,' Laura says, her hands in a surrender gesture.

We enter the kitchen, where I'm relieved to see that Kerry is in the garden with Niall. Hopefully she didn't overhear our conversation.

Laura slowly walks out to the garden.

'Hi, Kerry, how's everything?' Laura says, as she greets my alleged lover.

'I'm OK, apart from avoiding my bastard husband.'

'Pull up a chair and I'll get us a bottle of red.'

'For someone who's suspicious, you're very chummy with Kerry,' I tell Laura as she comes back into the kitchen.

'Can I open this bottle?' Laura asks, ignoring my remark.

'Sure.'

'There's something I need to tell you.'

Laura hesitates before continuing.

'For the past couple of months I've been ...'

Harry rushes into the kitchen.

'Dad swore at the doctors. It was amazing.'

'Why did you do that?' Laura asks me.

'Harry, dinner will be ready in five minutes. Why don't you log off the computer and wash your hands.'

'I'm on the case. Don't burn those sausages like you did on November the eleventh two thousand and ten. OK?' Harry remarks, before dashing off.

'Why did you swear?' Laura again enquires.

'The doctor told me that I've high blood pressure. I have to take tablets for it.'

'Oh, David, I'm sorry to hear that. How are you feeling right now?'

'I'm OK.'

'Tony, at work, has high blood pressure and he leads a perfectly normal life.'

'I know, I've been doing research on the Internet. I'll be fine, but I could do without it.'

Laura doesn't respond, so I continue.

'The doctor recommended more respite for Harry, to help me.'

'Harry hasn't got any worse lately, has he?'

'No, but ...'

'Surely you're not blaming Harry for your health problems?'

'Looking after Harry is adding to my stress, which in turn increases my blood pressure. Can you grasp that logic?' I sarcastically ask.

Laura closes her eyes and shakes her head.

'Thanks so much for your sympathy,' I add.

'What do you want me to do? Put my arm around you and encourage you to go ahead and send Harry to residential school?'

'There are other alternatives. Maybe boarding at his school once or twice a week? It'll be good for Harry, as well as us.'

'We've had this argument a hundred times, let's drop it right now, can we?'

Although I'm feeling agitated, I realise that this isn't the right time for this discussion.

A gentle tapping behind me grabs my attention. Niall is poking the oven, indicating that he is ready for dinner. Kerry is standing in the dining room, at a discreet distance, but watchful of Niall. She must have heard our argument.

'Thanks for reminding me,' I say to Niall.

Niall doesn't take his eyes off the oven.

'David, I can stay at Mum's tonight, it's not a problem,' Kerry discreetly remarks.

'No, don't be silly. Grab yourself a chair and I'll serve up.'

A couple of bottles of red wine later and the mood is more relaxed. The vintage two thousand and fifteen Oxford Landing, valued at five pounds and ninety-nine pence, goes down perfectly with our sausage and chips meal.

'Are you having two meals tonight?' Harry asks Kerry.

'No, I'm too full.'

'So, is Niall's dad going to eat yours and Niall's meals then?'

'I presume he's making his own. We don't live in the same house anymore.'

'Why, does he think that your house is shit?'

'No, we're just taking a break from each other.'

'Is it because he's fed up of Thomas?'

'Harry, that's enough questions for now,' I interrupt.

'I want to get a fish tank, with nine fishes in it,' Harry says; the master at changing the subject.

'I doubt that. Remember when we went to Jack's house? You took three of his fish out of the tank and they all died.'

'But I wanted to hug them.'

Jack is a neighbour. Needless to say we haven't been invited back.

'Harry, why don't you get your pyjamas on and get ready for bed?' Laura asks.

'OK, I wanna watch all of the *Big Brother* sleep programs,' Harry replies, before dashing off.

Harry has recorded all of the old *Big Brother* sleep programs. Each episode shows all the contestants sleeping and nothing else.

'It's bedtime for us as well, thanks for a lovely evening,' Kerry leans over and kisses me on the cheek, before taking Niall upstairs.

Laura takes another sip of wine. I'm anticipating a remark about the kiss, but for the next few minutes she is silent.

'It was only a friendly peck, nothing more,' I tell Laura.

'Was it? Oh, OK,' she says distractedly.

'Are you all right to drive back? You've had a few glasses.'

'I'm going to get a taxi. I'll pick my car up in the morning.'

'You can stay here. I'll sleep on the sofa.'

'What are your plans tomorrow?' she asks, ignoring my invitation.

'Kerry is leaving first thing in the morning and after that we've nothing on; why?'

'I couldn't get Maria to baby sit, but I'll still like to take you and Harry out for a meal; however it won't be just the three of us.'

I'm now feeling anxious, as Laura looks nervous.

'For the past couple of months I've been seeing someone.'

'Who?' is all I can mutter.

'His name is Sean. He's an accountant who comes into the office once a week. He got divorced three years ago and has two children – Timothy and Mary. He's kind and funny. I want you and Harry to meet him.'

Neither Laura nor I have been in a relationship since we separated; or so I thought.

'I presume he knows all about Harry?'

'Of course. Would it be OK if I bring Sean's kids along too?'

'Why didn't you tell me about Sean before now?'

'I wanted to see how things developed first.'

'And all along you were giving me a hard time about Kerry?'

'Sorry about that, maybe I was feeling guilty about Sean? I don't know.'

'What's Sean like?'

'He's lovely,' Laura says, with the most joyful expression that I have seen from her in years.

'You kept that quiet, but I'm delighted. I'd love to meet Sean and his family.'

We hug for a long, tender moment.

Thirty minutes later the taxi arrives.

'Say a prayer that it all goes well tomorrow,' Laura says, as she steps into the taxi.

'Don't worry. I'll bribe Harry with loads of Thomas presents.'

'I don't mind if he acts up, I just want everyone to get on.'

'It'll be fine. Go home and get some sleep.'

She kisses me goodbye. I feel sad that a part of me may be lost forever, but after all the torment that Laura has gone through, I couldn't be happier for her.

Sean, Timothy and Mary

Although Harry slept throughout the night, I didn't. I'm still coming to terms with Laura's relationship with Sean. How could I not see that coming? Am I so wrapped up in my own world that I didn't notice the increasing number of days when Laura couldn't baby sit Harry as she 'had something on?'

Since my divorce I've only been out on a couple of dates with a woman from work, but nothing serious. My broken marriage has made me reluctant to get involved in another relationship, even a short-term one. My responsibilities with Harry have always been my top priority, although this may be a get-out clause.

My friends and relatives are constantly asking about my love life. It would be great if I could find someone else, but I'm not ready for anything right now.

Six months before I met Laura, I had split up with Helen. We'd been going out for a year when I found out that she was sleeping with my friend Dominic. I got a text from Helen thanking me for the 'most wonderful evening and amazing sex'. The night in question I was watching England getting knocked out of the World Cup; yet again. David and Dominic are right next to each other in her contacts mobile listing. She confessed that she'd been with him for over two months. Despite Helen's willingness to finish with my so called friend,

I ended our relationship and never saw Dominic again. A mutual friend told me that Helen left him two weeks later.

A brief engagement with Caroline, a year with Helen and a twelve-year marriage to Laura is the summary of my love life to date.

I'm pleased, if surprised, that Laura has the strength to start another relationship, given what happened between us. But that was all in the past and she deserves some good fortune.

I pour another cup of coffee. Harry is in the living room watching the Disney channel. Although it's a risk, I decided against telling him all about our fellow diners tonight, as I want to minimise his confusion.

'You know that Grandma is coming over this morning?'

'Again?'

'Yes, and this time you'll be nice to her.'

'But she loves it when I squeeze her.'

'No, she hates it.'

'Why has she got white hair?'

'Because she's old.'

'It looks stupid. She should have black hair.'

The phone ringing interrupts our conversation.

'Hi, it's Alice here. I'm sorry for contacting you so early, but Bernadette has been onto me to ring you since I woke up. We've two spare tickets to see *Mamma Mia* tomorrow night and Bernadette is desperate for you and Harry to come with us. Our treat, of course.'

I'm immediately touched, not only by Alice's generosity, but also by Bernadette's invitation for Harry.

"That's a lovely gesture. However, I'm not sure if Harry could sit through two hours of Abba's songs.'

'It's always going to be a risk, but if it doesn't work out we can always leave. Bernadette loves "Dancing Queen", she plays that song about twenty times a day, but doesn't know any of the other Abba songs. Why don't you ask Harry?'

'OK, hold on a second.'

I walk into the living room.

'Harry, have you heard of Abba?'

'Just a little bit,' Harry says, using his thumb and middle finger.

'Bernadette wants you to see the *Mamma Mia* show tomorrow night. Do you want to go?'

'Can I have a margherita pizza as well?'

'Yes, we can go for a meal.'

'Count me in, Daddio.'

I'm surprised at how agreeable he is to the idea, but maybe that's due to the allure of Bernadette?

'He's up for it, but there's one condition. We go for a meal before the play and I'm paying.'

'Thanks, that'll be nice. How about meeting up outside Leicester Square tube at around six?'

'That's fine and thanks again for the invitation.'

That was unexpected, but I'm delighted all the same. I wonder who the other two tickets were meant for?

I'm also pleased that the friendship between Bernadette and Harry is developing.

I spend the next couple of hours updating my CV and looking for vacancies on the Internet. I contact one employment agency called EmployYou, who seem confident that 'despite my age' they'll be able to get me interviews fairly soon. I know that most of these people are full of crap, but it's reassuring that my qualifications and experience seem to be in demand. Only time will tell.

Soon after I get off the phone from the agency, my mother arrives.

Mum looks nervous, as she enters the hallway.

'Is Harry in?' she asks.

'He's upstairs in his room. Don't worry there will NOT be a repeat of the other day.'

'I hope not,' Mum replies, with a doubtful look.

A few minutes later, while we're having tea and biscuits in the kitchen, I can see the apprehension in my mother's eyes as she hears Harry come bounding down the stairs. I immediately get up to stand in front of her mimicking the urgency of a Secret Service agent when someone gets too close to the President.

'*Grandma*, come here and give me a hug,' Harry enthusiastically announces.

'Back off,' I reply, acting as a human shield around my mother. Am I taking the Secret Service role too seriously?

'Get him away from me,' Mum pleads.

Rather than being hurt by this remark it seems to have encouraged Harry, as he tries to push me out of the way.

'OK, everyone calm down. Now, Harry I want you to gently kiss Grandma.'

I hold Harry in a bear hug as he forcefully kisses his grandmother. Mum looks like she's been attacked by a murdering psychopath.

I position Harry at the other end of the kitchen table, but I still stand next to Mum.

'You must be gentle with Grandma. Can't you see that you're scaring her?' I ask my son.

'But she loves it.'

Somehow I cannot see Mum as being the masochist type.

'You've got to teach your son not to be so rough,' Mum tells me.

'I try, but it's not easy…'

'You should've disciplined him more when he was younger, then he wouldn't have these problems.'

I don't respond to this comment, although I want to.

'Harry, did you like my birthday present?' Grandma asks.

'No, it was a piece of crap.'

'That piece of crap cost me thirty-five pounds. I'll take it back if you don't want it.'

'OK,' Harry nonchalantly shrugs his shoulders.

'Mum, you know that Harry has no interest in clothes, but the jeans were great, he wore them yesterday.'

'What present would you like for next year then?' Mum enquires.

'No shitty jeans that's for sure, but don't worry about it because I think you'll be dead by then anyway.'

'Now you say sorry for Grandma for the remark,' I shout at my son, who seems obsessed with Mum's demise.

'David, don't worry. I've heard enough. I'll be off soon.'

'Grandma, do you like dicks?'

'What did you say?'

'All women like men's dicks, do you?'

'Get up to your room, *now*,' I demand.

Harry looks at his grandmother, still awaiting a reply, but when he realises that one isn't forthcoming he slowly walks out of the kitchen.

'There's no hope for that boy,' Mum says, ever diplomatic.

'Yes there is, Mum. I know he's got problems, but he can't help it. He was born into autism.'

'He's rude and violent and he's never going to do anything with his life.'

I'm tempted to tell my mother to get lost. What the hell does she know about bringing up an autistic child? Fiona and me were, by and large, good children. From about two years of age Harry has been extremely difficult. He was the main reason for my marriage failure and the stress of bringing him up continues to this day; to this minute. However I don't tell Mum my true feelings because I know how much that'll hurt her. She can say what the hell she likes, but I do not reciprocate.

'Are you going now?' is all that I come up with. Why do I walk on eggshells around my mother? I felt great sympathy for her when Dad passed away because they were so close, but why does that emotion override all of her faults?

'There's been no improvement in that boy for God knows how many years and the sooner you come to terms with that the better.'

'Mum, you can be so cruel. I want you to leave now.'

Mum looks at me and even she can see that I'm in no mood to discuss this any further. She walks into the hallway, has a quick look up the stairs and quietly leaves.

I'm angry at myself for not defending Harry more. After all, I stand up for him against strangers everyday.

Mum's visit puts me in a dark mood for the next couple of hours. However, Mum and Dad never understood autism, so I attempt to rationalise her behaviour from that perspective.

Later on my thoughts turn to the much anticipated evening with Sean and his family. It'll be strange seeing Laura with another man, but in true British tradition I'll keep my emotions in check.

At three minutes to six (a Harryism?) the doorbell rings.

'Hi, come in,' I say, as a nervous looking Laura walks past me.

Sean is standing on the driveway. He's tall, slim, dark-haired and dare I say it, good looking – damn it.

'You must be Sean?' I ask, stating the bleeding obvious. Laura's not the only anxious person.

'I'm pleased to finally meet you,' Sean eagerly shakes my hand, 'These are my two – Timothy and Mary.'

They both nod in my direction with less enthusiasm.

They enter the hallway and as I walk past the stairs I shout up to Harry.

'Mummy's friends are here. Come down and say hello.'

'It can wait. Batman is just about to kick the Joker's bollocks,' he calls out immediately.

This isn't the best of introductions.

'Get down *now*,' I reiterate.

'What the hell is going on?' Harry asks, upon his arrival.

'These are Mummy's new friends – Sean, Timothy and Mary.'

'And what do they want?'

'We've come to see you and your father. Then we're all going out for a meal,' Sean gently remarks.

'I want chips, burger and beans, OK? Now can I finish watching *Batman*?' Harry asks. I notice that Timothy and Mary are both stifling a giggle.

'Not just yet. We're going to sit in the living room and have a couple of drinks before we go to the restaurant,' Laura says.

'I'll have a Jack Daniels on the rocks,' Harry demands.

'That'll be a lemonade then,' Laura states.

'Do you like brown bread with marmalade?' Harry asks Timothy and Mary.

They both shake their heads.

'What about *Thomas the Tank Engine*?'

More shakes.

'But they like James Bond, is that right?' Laura enquires.

'Yeah, he's OK,' Timothy confirms.

'Someone should sack Daniel Craig. Pierce Brosnan was much better. He narrates Thomas.'

Timothy and Mary both laugh. I suspect that they're laughing at Harry, rather than with him.

'Why don't you like Thomas?' Harry asks.

'I used to, when I was about four,' Timothy immediately responds.

'Do you like Percy instead?'

'Let me get some drinks,' I interrupt, attempting to divert from the Thomas line of questioning.

Does Harry know that he's different from his peers? I once asked him what made him happy and he replied 'when I found a snail in our garden.' He then told me that he put it into a Sainsburys bag and let it fend for itself on Streatham High Road because it was 'bored living in our garden'.

Fifteen minutes later Timothy and Mary are watching some teenage television programme, while Sean is talking to Harry.

'How are you getting on at school?' Sean asks.

'Mister Bremner is a prick'.

'OK. Who is he?'

'A prick.'

'What's your favourite lesson?' Sean asks, seemingly undaunted by Harry's abrupt responses.

'I like it when we have sausage and mash on Tuesdays.'

'I'm sure that you have plenty of friends at school?'

'Bernadette is my fifth best friend.'

Sean glances at Laura, who shakes her head, indicating do not pursue a 'is she your girlfriend?' type of conversation.

'All the children make too much noise and it drives me crazy.'

'You don't like noise?'

'Noise is a heap of shit.'

Half an hour later we arrive at a Harvester restaurant in Streatham. Harry is sitting in between Mary and Timothy. After ordering our meal Sean goes up to the bar to get the drinks.

'So, what's the verdict on Sean?' Laura asks me.

'I like him. He's warm and friendly. You're well matched.'

'Thanks, David.'

'He's also making a big effort to talk to Harry.'

'How do you think the kids are getting along?'

'That's always going to be more difficult, but so far so good.'

'What do you think of Justin Timberlake?' Mary asks Harry.

Harry merely stares back at her. Mary glances at Timothy before asking again.

'Do you like Justin Timberlake?'

'Is he your milkman?'

Sean's children immediately burst into laughter. I'm just about to intervene when Laura puts her hand on my arm.

'Our milkman is Pete Bell. He's fifty-two years old and is a bit of a bastard. He has no hair. Does Timberlake have any hair?'

More laughter greets Harry's question.

'Yes, Timberlake does have hair,' confirms Mary, giving no indication to the real identity of their 'milkman'.

'Harry, Justin Timberlake is not a milkman, he's a singer,' I say.

Timothy and Mary look disappointed, rather than embarrassed.

'Is everyone having a good time? I heard laughter, which is a good sign,' Sean cheerfully remarks, upon his return.

Tight smiles greet his observation.

The meal arrives shortly afterwards.

'Your mummy tells me that you're playing at the Royal Festival Hall. That's going to be amazing,' Sean comments.

Harry looks up, but focuses on the contents of Sean's plate.

'What song are you going to be singing?'

'Dunno, some piece of crap.'

'Harry, Sean is talking politely to you, please stop being rude,' Laura sternly tells her son.

'But why do I have to keep practising the same song over and over again? It's wasting my energy.'

'You should feel privileged to be singing at such an important venue. All the great singers have played there.'

'Pierce Brosnan hasn't and he's the best singer ever. Haven't you seen *Mamma Mia*?'

Nobody answers that.

'Why can't we have the concert at our house?'

'You might have some difficulty getting the twenty-five piece orchestra into the living room,' Laura points out.

'They could play on the roof.'

An orchestra on the roof and the choir in the front garden – that would be sure to attract the local newspapers.

'Do you have a dog?' Harry asks Timothy.

'No.'

'I hate it when they bark. Why do they do that?'

Timothy shrugs his shoulders.

'Are they angry when they bark?' Harry enquires.

Timothy smiles at this remark.

'Our cat meows when she wants food or when I hug her too tightly.'

Timothy and Mary are now both laughing.

Harry then grabs a handful of chips from Timothy's plate and stuffs them straight in his mouth.

'What the fuck are you doing?' Timothy angrily enquires.

'That's enough of that talk,' Sean immediately retorts.

'But he's a fucking idiot.'

'Do you understand that Harry is autistic?' I shout at Timothy.

He doesn't respond.

'I said, do you know that Harry is autistic?'

'Yeah, Dad told me,' he condescending replies.

'Have you any idea what autism is?'

'It means that he's a bit mental.'

I stand up and walk over to Timothy.

'Don't you *ever* say that about my son again.'

My face is now only a few inches away from his.

He looks at me, but doesn't reply.

'Did you get the picture?' I shout, even louder.

'Yeah.'

His response is less defiant this time.

'I noticed you and Mary sniggering at everything Harry was saying. If I ever catch you laughing or insulting my son again I'll...'

'OK, David, calm down. Let's move Harry over here,' Laura interrupts.

She's right, I've made my point and it'll be meaningless to continue with my tirade.

Harry is now sitting in between Laura and me. He continued to eat his dinner throughout my outburst, and didn't even look at Timothy when he made his comments.

'David, I can't apologise enough. Rest assured Timothy will be punished,' Sean explains.

He looks sympathetically at me, before turning to Timothy.

'You won't receive any pocket money or be allowed out to socialise with your yobbo friends for the next six weeks. Do I make myself clear?' Sean firmly tells his son.

'Yes.'

'Sean, this type of situation happens a lot. Maybe I overreacted.'

'You reacted the way any father would when their son was being abused. This will *not* happen again.'

I discreetly look at Laura, whose eyes are watering. What a difficult situation she's in. Sean's obviously a nice man, but with Sean comes two stroppy teenagers.

The rest of the meal passes without any further incident.

Outside the restaurant a more subdued Timothy and Mary climb into their father's car, without so much as a goodbye.

'David, it was lovely meeting you and Harry. I hope that the earlier incident will not stop us getting together again,' Sean tells me, as he shakes my hand.

'Not at all. It'll be nice to meet up for a drink one night, without the sprogs,' I reply.

'Sounds good. Harry, I'm sorry that Timothy got annoyed with you.'

'What do you do during the day?' Harry asks Sean, apparently unaware of Sean's apology.

'Do you mean what job do I have?'

As Harry doesn't respond I nod on his behalf.

'I'm an accountant, I add up numbers.'

'Miss Brandon is our Maths teacher. She always wears short skirts and has big breasts.'

'OK, Harry, that's enough information about Miss Brandon. Now say goodbye to Sean,' I tell my son.

'Have you got green carpets in your house?' Harry asks Sean.

'I don't think so,' Sean replies, still thinking about the question.

'I've a green carpet in my bedroom and I like that.'

'Would you like to come to our house?' Sean enquires.

'I'll only go if you don't put that sickly *Coronation Street* on the telly.'

'OK, that's a deal.' Sean offers his hand, but Harry looks at the pavement instead.

'Harry is not good at handshakes,' I inform Sean.

'No problem, I hope to see you soon,' Sean tells us before getting into his car.

Laura approaches me. 'I'm going back with Sean.'

'OK, I'm sorry for losing my temper earlier. I …'

'David, I was seconds away from saying exactly the same thing. Sean's mortified.'

'We live in a cocoon with Harry, and forget how hard normal teenagers can be,' I say.

'I so wanted all the kids to get along. That's going to be difficult now,' a tearful Laura reflects.

'Children simply react to what they see, they haven't got the wherewithal to understand Harry's shortcomings,' I try to explain.

We embrace. Laura's relationship with Sean seems to have brought us closer together.

'Please don't worry.'

Laura smiles at me. She then kisses Harry goodbye, before heading off in Sean's car.

On the car journey home I put on a Sinatra CD to help ease my fragile nerves.

'Who's this?' Harry asks, with a facial expression of someone who has just stepped into dog poo.

'Frank Sinatra.'

'Where does he live?'

'He's dead.'

'So what's the point of playing his music?'

'Harry, I don't know how many times that I've told you, but when we go to a restaurant you *do not* steal anybody else's food.'

'But Timothy had twenty-eight chips and I only had twenty-one.'

'I don't care if Timothy had a hundred chips. If you want more then ask me and I'll order another portion. It's as simple as that.'

'But why did he have more chips than me?'

'Just drop it.'

Harry doesn't respond.

'Did you like Timothy and Mary?'

'They're morons. Why don't they like Thomas?'

'Not everyone likes Thomas. Apart from that, were they OK with you?'

'No, because Timothy had more chips than me.'

'What about Sean?'

'He has a weird voice, is he from earth?'

'Yes, he's Irish, just like Grandma and Grandpa.'

Harry looks perplexed.

'So, what did you think of Sean?'

Harry merely shrugs his shoulders.

'Mummy likes him,' I add.

'Does he take his underpants off for Mummy?'

'That's private between Mummy and Sean. I do know that Mummy is happy when she is with Sean.'

I'm assuming that Harry is talking about sex, but I'm not sure. I decide not to pursue the conversation as Harry has mentally switched off. He's flicking through the yellow pages, which is a permanent fixture in our car.

Twenty minutes later I'm lying alongside Harry in his bed. It's been another exhausting day and I hope that Harry is equally tired.

'Do you think that you could become friends with Timothy and Mary?' I ask.

'Nah, they don't like Thom...'

'Thomas, yes I know. What about Sean?'

'Only when he speaks properly.'

'OK, let's get some sleep now. Goodnight, son.'

I lean over to kiss his forehead.

Within minutes I drift off to sleep.

The sound of water running in the bathtub wakes me up. I glance at the alarm clock and it's two fifty-four. The cleanest boy in Streatham is having his nightly bath.

Mamma Mia

It's another five-thirty start time for breakfast the following morning. After breakfast Harry goes into the living room to watch TV, while I'm contemplating last night's incident with Timothy. I'll always defend my son, so I've no qualms about saying what I did to him, but I do regret the stress that this has caused Laura. There will now be doubts in her mind about any long-term relationship with Sean. Why are a lot of today's teenagers moody, aggressive and devoid of respect?

Almost telepathically, Laura rings.

'How's Harry?' she asks.

'He's looking at the *Bottom* DVD that Robert got him for his birthday.'

'Is that the Rik Mayall show?'

'Yeah, there're a few swear words in it, but don't worry, I'll monitor the situation,' I add.

'How are you?' I ask.

'Depressed. Yesterday didn't go so well, did it?'

'Yeah, it was upsetting.'

'Sean was absolutely furious and read them the riot act on the way home. I don't expect them to have the maturity of an adult, but I wanted them to be nice to Harry, that's not too much to ask, is it?'

By the time we finish our conversation Laura's in a better mood. I wasn't lying when I told Laura that

I liked Sean, but I still can't get used to the fact she's moving on from me. Because neither of us have been involved in a relationship since our split I subconsciously thought that we hadn't got over each other. However, it looks like Laura has.

For the rest of the day I catch up on my housework, while Harry sits in front of the TV. As the doctor suggested, I aim to get myself in shape by going out running. I've been meaning to do this for a couple of years. When I first thought of this crazy idea I knew that it would have to be carefully coordinated around Laura's availability, but then in another moment of madness I somehow convinced myself that Harry could run with me. Despite his lack of physical exertion he always does well in the school sports day. I'm certain that he'll not greet my suggestion with too much enthusiasm. Hopefully it'll burn off some of that nervous energy and he might even sleep better. While on the subject of pie in the sky suggestions my last wish is that Christopher Biggins will become the next Prime Minister.

Harry walks into the kitchen.

'Daddy, after I sing that shit song are all those people going to clap?'

'I hope so.'

'But it's going to make too much noise.'

'Yes, but it'll be a good noise because everyone will be happy to hear you sing.'

'I don't like noise, can't you get rid of it everywhere?'

'It's not as simple as that.'

'I'm not going to do the concert if there's any clapping.'

I don't recall any pop star pulling out of a concert for that reason.

I'm not sure that it was a good decision to ask Harry to do this concert. Still, what I have got to be nervous about? There'll only be two and a half thousand people there on Saturday.

At six o'clock we catch the one fifty-nine bus from Streatham to Brixton. As we approach the Brixton tube station, Harry gives me the journey breakdown.

'On the Victoria line, after Brixton, we'll go through Stockwell, Vauxhall, Pimlico, Victoria and Green Park. We'll then change onto the Piccadilly line for Piccadilly Circus and Leicester Square. The Victoria line is a light blue colour and the Piccadilly line is a dark blue colour.'

Perhaps Harry should apply for a London Underground travel guide, if such a job exists?

We get a ticket at the tube station and jump on a train.

Alice and Bernadette are waiting for us at the Leicester Square tube station and we then walk to a nearby Pizza restaurant. Amazingly, the meal passes without any major incident. Alice is pleasant company, while Bernadette and Harry talk incessantly about the wellbeing of Thomas, Percy, Edward and the rest of the Thomas clan.

On the way to the theatre, Bernadette starts singing 'Dancing Queen' and Harry enthusiastically joins in.

'OK, kids, let's save the rest of the song for the show,' Alice wearily remarks, sounding like she has heard Bernadette sing this song once or twice before.

As Harry also confessed to knowing little about Abba, I'm beginning to think that there might be a Thomas connection here.

'Harry, which Thomas DVD has "Dancing Queen" in it?' I ask.

'*The Tribute to Rosie* video.'

'Who's Rosie?'

'Rosie is a purple engine with red wheels. She loves Thomas, but Thomas gets annoyed when she follows him. However, when he has an accident, Rosie helps him, which makes Thomas respect her. She was first shown in the tenth series of *Thomas*.'

'Thanks for that comprehensive update,' I say.

Alice and I glance at each other and a smile is shared, as the Abba/Thomas connection is revealed.

At the theatre we settle into our seats. I'm concerned that we're three rows from the front. Is this too close for comfort?

Bernadette and Harry are still singing *Dancing Queen* after the show has started.

'Harry, please be quiet. You're disturbing everyone,' I say.

'But why are they not playing "Dancing Queen"? They're talking too much and the other songs are for idiots.'

'Harry, I am *not* going to tell you again, please keep your voice down.'

'Get on with it, you bunch of bastards,' Harry shouts.

A couple of actors even look in our direction and I hear some murmurings amongst the audience.

'Do you want to leave now?' I ask, as quietly as possible, as I feel several hundred pairs of eyes staring at us.

Harry doesn't respond, but thankfully keeps quiet.

Within seconds a security guard crouches down next to me.

'If your son doesn't stop interrupting the show, you'll both have to leave.'

'I'm sorry, but my boy can't help it, he's autistic.'

'Come on, you shits, sing "Dancing Queen",' Bernadette shouts.

The security guard looks up and must wonder what the hell's going on.

'She's autistic as well,' I explain.

Bernadette's outburst further unsettles the audience. The guard crouches next to Alice and no doubt gives her a similar warning.

Bernadette and Harry both stand up to continue their singing duet.

This time the audience start booing and the show actually stops.

'That's it, you'll have to go,' came the inevitable response from the guard. Thrown out after only eight minutes, that must be a record for the Novella theatre.

Unfortunately the exit door is at the back of the theatre, so we have to run the gauntlet of the disgruntled audience – 'you're a disgrace', 'piss off', 'can't you control your brats?' were only a few of the insults coming our way.

'We simply cannot tolerate this behaviour. I'm afraid that you'll not be allowed back in to watch the rest of the show,' one of the group of theatre employees explains to us in the foyer.

'As you already know, my daughter and her friend Harry are both autistic and simply don't have the appropriate social skills,' Alice explains.

'Then why did you put them into a situation like this?' the same man asks.

'What do you expect us to do, keep them locked inside our house all day? How dare you tell me what social activities my daughter can or cannot attend. I should fucking report you.'

Anxious looks are exchanged between the group, as they fear a potential hot potato.

'If you contact our Customer Services department and mention my name a refund will be made,' a senior looking man tells Alice, as he hands her his card.

'As opposed to tickets for another night?' Alice enquires.

'You can exchange tickets for another performance, but again I must stress that shouting in the middle of a performance is unacceptable.'

'A refund is fine, thanks,' I interrupt, hoping to bring this episode to a close.

Alice accepts the card. Meanwhile Harry hands the same man a piece of paper.

'Is this your address?' the man asks.

'Can that lot come around to our house tomorrow night and sing "Dancing Queen"?' Harry asks, pointing to the exit door, the other side of which the show has hopefully resumed.

'Our house is in Streatham. If you get on at Leicester Square and go on the Piccadilly line ...'

'OK, Harry, let's get going,' I intervene, taking the piece of paper off the bemused man.

'My dad will make chips and fish fingers for everyone,' Harry adds, although I'm not sure that this offering will swing the balance in our favour.

'At least you didn't lose out financially,' I say to Alice, attempting in vain to put a positive slant on this disaster.

'That arsehole back there really pissed me off,' Alice replies.

'*Why* did you have to keep on singing that stupid fucking song?' she asks her daughter.

It's ironic that Alice was reprimanding me for my language yesterday and now she's swearing like a trooper. Given her state of mind I decide against mentioning this to her, even in jest.

'They must've forgotten to sing it, so I was helping them to remember,' Bernadette responds.

'Yeah, they kept on singing about their mother, who gives a shit about that?' Harry adds.

'I know this is disappointing, but we half expected it,' I tell Alice.

Alice looks at the pavement, but doesn't respond.

'It's nice that Bernadette and Harry are spending some time together. They seem to like each other.'

Alice now looks up at me.

'I know, but I really thought that she would enjoy the whole show. She loves music.'

'Let's go to a pub, we both need a drink.'

She smiles at me, gently takes Bernadette's hand and we all head off to the nearest West End pub.

'If they're not going to come to our house tomorrow, can we see the show again next week?' Harry asks.

'We'll give it a miss for a while,' I reply, not wishing to put Alice and me through another evening of hell.

After being rejected from three West End pubs because they wouldn't allow children, we end up in our local pub in Streatham.

'Being thrown out of three pubs and one theatre, that's not bad going for an evening,' I tell a more relaxed Alice.

'That has to be the most embarrassing moment of my life, and I've had a few,' Alice responds, before taking another sip of her red wine.

The barman collects the empty glasses from our table.

'Have a happy summer, my friend,' Harry addresses the barman. Harry loves the Happy Christmas and Happy New Year greetings so much that he extends this to happy autumn, winter, spring and summer. The barman looks at Harry sceptically. I don't bother to fill in the gaps.

'Yeah, that's right, you have a wonderful summer, young man. The weather today was seventy-three degrees Fahrenheit, tomorrow it will be seventy-eight degrees Fahrenheit, Wednesday it's going to be eighty-two degrees Fahrenheit, Thursday it'll be …'

'Bernadette, we get the idea,' interrupts Alice.

'But the weathermen are a bunch of losers. On Saturday they said that it was going to be sixty-nine degrees Fahrenheit for today. They're a fucking disgrace.'

'Bernadette, *please* do not swear,' Alice reprimands her daughter.

'She's only following her mother's lead,' I eventually have the courage to remark, albeit in a light-hearted tone.

'Yes, I did lose it back there,' Alice ruefully smiles.

'I don't like your fingernails. They're too long and dirty,' Harry informs the barman.

'Are you taking the piss?' an increasingly agitated barman enquires.

'Just cut them. My dad cuts mine, which makes me feel a bit sick. Do you want him to do yours?'

Before the barman responds, I step in.

'I'm sorry, my son is autistic.'

The barman's tense expression eases, as he nods his response.

'Harry, was that chap a bit mad?' Bernadette asks, as the barman walks away.

'Yeah, I want to kick his arse up to the ceiling. Why the hell does he have long fingernails?'

'Maybe he doesn't look at his fingernails everyday and doesn't know how long they are?' Bernadette enquires.

'Good point. And why are all the Streatham buses all red? It's madness,' Harry asks.

'Shit knows.'

'Why don't they make them all pink with yellow and orange triangles?'

'Yeah, that would be better. All the buses smell like horse's piss anyway.'

This reminds me of the time I painted Harry's bedroom sky blue. While I was sleeping Harry even skipped his early morning bath to paint the bananas, apples and oranges all sky blue because he didn't like their original colours. He also ate two of the newly painted apples before I woke up.

'Harry, would you like to see the Powerpuff Girls film in the cinema with me?' Bernadette asks.

'Do they save the world before bedtime again?'

'Oh yeah, they kick some serious butt.'

'Then count me in, baby.'

Alice and I look at each other. I think we're both feeling the same overwhelming joyous emotion. I can see the tears running down Alice's cheeks. She quickly searches through her handbag, presuming looking for a tissue. I divert my attention away from her to mini-mise any further embarrassment. These past few days have been a roller coaster of emotions, but this has to be one of the greatest moments of my life. To any parent of 'normal' children this may seem like a ridiculously over-the-top statement, but autistic children rarely form a relationship with the opposite sex, so our expectation levels are extremely low, if non-existent. For Harry to go on a date, no matter what the nature of the date may be, is a momentous occasion. I'm so happy and proud for my boy.

For the next couple of minutes there is silence before I finally speak.

'That was a bit forward of your daughter.'

'I suppose so, but if we had to wait for Harry to make a move...'

'Point taken. Obviously one or both of us will have to accompany them.'

'I think that it'll seem more like a date if only one of us goes. We'll decide nearer the time. Bernadette has so few friends, I'm so delighted for them both.'

'Do you think that they might hang around for more than eight minutes at the cinema?'

We both laugh, which is a lovely way to end a stress-ful evening.

'Why didn't they let us watch those clowns singing "Dancing Queen"?' Harry asks, on the bus ride back from the pub.

'Because you were disturbing all the other people by singing and shouting.'

'Didn't those idiots on the stage want to sing "Dancing Queen"?'

'They *were* going to sing that song a bit later.'

'But they were wasting my time.'

This conversation is going around in circles.

'The next time Bernadette comes around you both can sing "Dancing Queen" as many times as you like.'

Although personally speaking I don't ever want to hear that song ever again.

'Are you looking forward to seeing the Powerpuff Girls films with Bernadette?'

Harry stares ahead, without acknowledging my question.

'Harry, are you looking forward to watching the film?'

'As long as the film doesn't last longer than two hours and four minutes.'

'Do you like Bernadette?'

'She's OK when she doesn't laugh or make too much noise.'

I suppose that's as good enough endorsement as any.

'What do you want to do tomorrow?'

'Let's look in the sky for aeroplanes.'

'OK, but planes don't often fly above Streatham. Do you want to go to Heathrow airport instead?'

'Nah, I don't like all those suitcases. I want to see the Streatham planes.'

'OK, Streatham planes it is.'

A few minutes later my mobile rings.

'Hi David, Clarence here from EmployYou. I'm sorry to bother you so late, but we've got an interview at Lloyds for ten o'clock tomorrow morning. Can you make it?'

'Er, yeah, I think so.'

'I told you that I'd produce the goods for you, didn't I?'

'Yes, that's good news.'

'I've a few guidelines for you that'll almost certainly result in a successful interview. Act confident, even fucking arrogant, the city people lap that up. Give the impression that you're doing them a favour, not the other way around. Pretend that you've another interview lined up, a person in demand is always more desirable. False smiles are a must and firm handshakes are essential. Do I need to go on?'

Shut the fuck up, you stupid prick.

'That's enough for now,' I reply.

I take down all the details, before getting off the bus.

Twenty minutes later when I'm lying in bed next to Harry and I suddenly thought – who's going to look after my son tomorrow?

Job Interview

As Laura, Kerry and Alice are all working today I'm left with little option but to take Harry with me to the interview. This will hardly impress the shy and retiring Clarence, so I simply don't tell him.

This is far from ideal, but once again highlights the difficulties in getting respite care for a special needs child. I could have asked my sister to look after Harry, but I'd rather cancel the interview. Fiona's nervousness and inability to cope with Harry isn't a bad reflection on her. I'd only allow another parent of an autistic child or a special needs carer to look after my son and nearly all the parents of Harry's friends feel the same.

'Where are we going?' Harry asks, as we board the London Victoria train.

'I've a job interview for Lloyds bank in London.'

Harry stares out of the window, seemingly uninterested in my response.

'I have to change my job,' I add, attempting to simplify this conversation.

'Why don't they sell chips and steak and kidney pies at the banks?'

'I'm not sure, but I'll suggest that at the interview.'

'And why do the people at the bank always talk through the windows?'

'The windows are there in case someone steals the bank's money,' I respond.

'Do the bank people live behind those windows?'

'No, they've all got their own houses.'

Although a banking commune sounds interesting.

'Harry, when we're at the bank I *do not* want you to swear, fart, talk about Thomas, milkmen, wasps, bees or sing "Dancing Queen". If you're quiet I'll buy you two DVDs on the way home, OK?'

'Are there going to be any kids at the bank?'

'No.'

'So it's just fat and bald men and women?'

'I don't think there'll be too many bald women, although you never know. Harry, this is important to me, so *please* be good.'

'Why do those bank people always shout "*next please*"? I want to kill them when they do that.'

Conversations with Harry can be extremely stressful.

'Mrs Prior said that there are a lot of gang fights in London. I hope that I don't get my shoes stolen.'

'Rest assured, your shoes won't be stolen.'

'Do we have to join a gang when we get off at Victoria station?' my son asks.

'No, it's not compulsory.'

'Good. I don't want to get the shit kicked out of me.'

'Harry, how many times do I have to tell you? There is nothing to be afraid of in London.'

'So nobody is going to bite my bollocks?'

'No, you'll be fine, but *please* cut down on the swearing.'

I make a mental note to ask Mrs Prior about the contents of her gang warfare lesson.

'So are you going to be a good boy?'

'How long are we going to be there?' Harry asks, ignoring my question.

'I don't know, maybe an hour.'

'I've brought my stopwatch, so when it's sixty minutes and one second we'll leave.'

'OK,' I optimistically respond.

I have a technical test, followed by an interview with a Project Manager. According to Clarence I'm the first to be interviewed and the whole process shouldn't take longer than forty-five minutes. If true, this will satisfy Harry's timescales.

'Can we go to Ringo Starr's house in Beverley Hills for Christmas?' Harry asks.

"Harry, we don't know Ringo personally, so we can't just invite ourselves to his house,' I reply, although I wouldn't say no to tea and sandwiches at Paul McCartney's gaff.

'Ringo will love it. I bet he's got hundreds of Thomas toys in his house.'

'Sorry, Harry, we can't do that.'

Harry looks perplexed.

'There are too many people on this train,' my son remarks, changing the subject.

'That's because everyone is going into London to work.'

'They must be idiots. Why don't they stay at home and watch *Scooby Do*?'

'They go to work to earn some money.'

'The banks have loads of cash, why don't they go there instead? You can tell them the address, can't you?'

'The banks don't give money out to everyone, you have to put some money in there first.'

'If I get some ten pound notes there's no way I'm giving it to the bank; the greedy bastards.'

As usual, this chat is going around in circles.

'Do you like grass?' Harry asks a man, opposite us.

'What do you mean?' he asks.

'You know; grass.'

The man understandably looks confused.

'Didn't your daddy teach you about grass when you were younger?'

'You mean drugs?'

'What the hell are you talking about? Grass is what we walk on.'

'Oh, OK.'

'Well, do you like it?'

'It's alright,' he replies.

'I love it and so do my feet, because it's much softer than walking on the pavement.'

'I see.'

I doubt that he does.

'Ants live in the grass and they think that it's great. They're my favourite animal.'

'OK, Harry, that's enough about grass.'

I don't bother to explain Harry's autism, as I'm trying to read Clarence's note's on Lloyds.

The man looks at me, and then Harry, before continuing to read his newspaper.

Half an hour later me and Harry are waiting in the Lloyds bank reception area.

'Remember what I told you about being good?' I ask my son.

Harry doesn't respond and continues to read his London A-Z, which I'm told is a fascinating book. I don't pursue the conversation as he's now quiet and that's all I can wish for this morning. He glances at his stopwatch. We've already used twelve minutes of the allocated sixty.

My last interview, at Homely Insurance was thirteen years ago, so I'm a little out of practice, and Clarence's bullshit guidance was no use to man or beast. I want to make a good impression; my mortgage depends on it.

An attractive lady approaches me.

'David McCarthy?' she asks.

I nod, then stand up to shake her hand.

'My name is Emma. I'm sorry I'm late, we've had problems with a couple of PCs, that need rebuilding; can you help me on this?'

'That's not really my expertise, I …'

'Don't worry, I'm only joking. I wouldn't be that cruel,' she replies, with a confident smile.

An IT Project Manager with a sense of humour is rare, if not extinct.

'Shall we get started?' she asks.

'I couldn't get a babysitter today, so I've had to bring my son along,' I nervously tell Emma.

She looks over my shoulder at Harry.

'That's OK, he'll be fine here. We shouldn't take longer than forty-five minutes. The receptionist will keep an eye out for him.'

'It's not as simple as that. Harry is autistic, so I can't leave him alone.'

'Does that mean that he has to be with us for the interview?'

The penny's dropped.

'Yes. If I didn't bring him along I would've cancelled the interview and this is too good an opportunity to miss.'

I can still turn on the charm, when need be.

'This is the first time that I've interviewed a father and son together, but I understand your circumstances, so let's go.'

'Harry, this is Emma. She's going to interview me.'

'Does that mean that you're going to have sex?' Harry asks.

Emma looks embarrassed.

'I'm sorry, Emma, I just need a minute with Harry.'

She nods, as I pull him to one side.

'If you are rude one more time then *all* of your DVDs are going to the charity shop this afternoon, is that clear?'

'Daddy, why is your face so red? It's normally pink.'

'When we're in the room with Emma I don't want to hear one more word from you, OK?'

'I'm just trying to enjoy myself.'

A couple of minutes later the three of us are sitting in a tiny room. Harry is in the corner, still reading his London A-Z.

'I apologise for Harry's behaviour, he doesn't understand ...'

'There's no need to apologise. It must be extremely difficult for you looking after a special needs child while holding down a highly pressurised job.'

That doesn't sound too promising, or am I reading too much into it?

'Shall we start with the technical test?' she asks.

She hands me three pages of technical questions and tells me that she'll be back in twenty minutes. A quarter of an hour later I'm finished and feel confident about my answers.

Harry has been quiet throughout and I'm tempted to praise him, but this often backfires. A couple of months ago Laura and I attended a parent/teacher evening with Harry at his school. As we were leaving I commented on his good behaviour, to which he replied, 'Yeah, and I didn't even call Mister O'Shea a fat moron.' The problem was Mister O'Shea was walking right in front of us and turned around to confirm the source of that remark. Needless to say he gave Harry low grades for English and commented that although Harry has good language skills, he tends to favour the words that you can't find in a dictionary.

Emma returns and wastes no time starting the interview.

'Why do you want to join Lloyds?' she asks.

'Lloyds is a world-renowned company. Its IT division has a cutting edge technology, which will give me a great opportunity to further develop my technical skills.'

She smiles in response. Is it a false smile or does she really believe all my crap?

'Have you any ambitions to move into management?'

I look over at Harry, who continues to read his *London A-Z*. Is he studying to be a London cabbie?

'I'm sorry, what was the question?'

'Have you any plans to go into management?' she asks.

'Not yet. I want to initially concentrate on the technical aspect of the job, but management is my long-term aim,' I lie, attempting to sound ambitious.

'Fifty-two minutes and thirty-seven seconds gone,' Harry says.

Emma and I look at Harry.

'You've seven minutes and twenty-three, no twenty-two, no twenty-one seconds left, so hurry up,' Harry adds.

'Remember what I said about the DVDs?' I remind my son.

'Why do you both keep talking about shit?'

'One more word from you and your DVDs are gone,' I shout at Harry.

'Mister McCarthy, can we continue?' Emma despairingly enquires.

'Of course, again I apologise.'

'What are your strengths?' Emma asks.

'I have a strong technical background and I work well under pressure.'

Emma raises an eyebrow, given my last outburst.

'This place sucks,' Harry declares.

'Harry, I'm talking to your dad for only a few more minutes and then you'll be free to leave,' Emma tells Harry.

'How much did you pay for your tits?' Harry asks.

'I beg your pardon?'

'Your breasts are massive, you must've bought them from a shop. Robert's mum did. He thinks that she got them from WH Smiths and they cost her nine pounds and ninety-nine pence.'

'That's it, the interview is over. David, I appreciate that your son is autistic, but I simply cannot tolerate this behaviour; I'm sorry,' Emma says, clearly upset.

'No, it's me who should apologise.'

I stand up to shake her hand. I've seen her bewildered expression many times, in reaction to another one of Harry's outbursts.

'Come on, we're going,' I tell Harry.

'Oh good, it's only been fifty-four minutes and thirteen seconds. Well done for leaving before time.'

I storm out of the office, leaving Harry struggling to keep up. After walking for several minutes I sit down on a bench and soon after Harry joins me.

'Why couldn't you keep that big mouth of yours shut?' I shout at Harry.

'But I wanted to find out if she got her tits in the same shop as Stephanie. I wasn't being rude.'

I'm not in the mood to pursue this conversation so we immediately head home. On the train journey I reflect on the past hour. Up to Harry's interruption I thought that I was doing well at the interview, even feeling confident. To be able to secure another job position so soon after being made redundant would have been perfect, but in an instant Harry changed that.

I'm still angry by the time we arrive home. The first thing that I do is grab a dozen Thomas the Tank Engine DVDs.

'Are you going to watch Thomas today?' Harry asks.

'No, I've got a better use for them.'

We get back in the car and drive the short distance to the Cancer Research charity shop. I place the Sainsbury's bag, full of DVDs, onto the shop counter.

'These DVDs are a donation,' I tell the elderly shop assistant.

She glances inside the bag.

'Thanks, that's generous of you,' she says.

As we're walking out of the shop Harry stops me.

'When will the old fart be finished watching my DVDs?' he asks.

'The DVDs are not for her. They are for the charity shop, who will sell them. They are no longer yours.'

'What the hell's going on?'

'I told you what would happen if you didn't behave yourself at the bank, didn't I?'

'But you can't give away my DVDs. I love Thomas,' Harry pleads.

'I *am* giving away your DVDs and that's final,' I tell him.

Harry starts to cry and approaches the shop assistant.

'Excuse me, old woman, can I have my DVDs back please?'

By now everyone in the shop is staring as us, thinking that I'm a total bastard for giving away my son's DVDs and nonchalantly dismissing his compassionate appeal for their return. Yes, I'm officially the pantomime villain. However, for once I'm following up on my earlier threat; how else will Harry learn that there are repercussions for his bad behaviour?

'Daddy, what am I going to with my life without my DVDs?'

All eyes in the shop are focused on me.

'Come on, let's go,' I firmly tell him.

He turns around to face the shop assistant.

'Old broads don't like Thomas, so please give them back to me.'

The lady looks like she's weakening, so I usher Harry out of the shop.

'Get in the car now. That'll teach you not to be rude.'

Harry reluctantly walks to the car, turning around every few steps in the hope that the lady changed her mind. As we drive away Harry rests his head against the car window to stare, through tear-filled eyes, at the Cancer Research shop.

An hour later I'm sitting in my garden having a cup of tea, although it did cross my mind to get the whisky bottle out. Despite feeling good earlier about sticking to my principles, I'm now regretting my action. I was extremely angry coming out of the interview, but for fifty-two minutes and thirty-seven seconds Harry was immaculately behaved; of course that couldn't last. I was setting him up for failure by putting him in that impossible position.

I walk upstairs to his bedroom and can still hear him sobbing before I enter.

'Harry, are you OK?'

Silly question really.

'Why didn't that bird at the bank just tell me where she brought her tits?'

I sit on his bed.

'Harry, you must understand that you cannot ask a woman about her breasts, it's very private.'

'Then why did she make them so big?'

'It doesn't matter if they are big or small, you cannot talk about it, OK?'

Harry stares at the carpet, with a perplexed expression.

'Let's go back up to the charity shop to see if any of your DVDs are left.'

Before I finish the sentence Harry dashes out of the bedroom, nearly jumps down the stairs and straight into the car.

Ten minutes later the door of the Cancer Research shop bursts open and Harry strides up to the shop assistant, who is a middle-aged man.

'Where's that lady? She better not have died because I want my Thomas DVDs back.'

'Let me explain,' I say, 'we came here an hour ago and handed in some Thomas the Tank Engine DVDs, but I've made a mistake and need them back. Are there any left?'

'I've only just started, but I did sell a Thomas DVD a couple of minutes ago.'

'That old bat couldn't have seen all the DVDs already. Why did you give them all away? Are you fucked up in your brain?' Harry shouts at the man.

'Harry, *please* do not speak to the man like that.'

My son is too wound up to listen to me.

'I'm so sorry, he's autistic,' I tell the man.

That line has become my catch phase.

The shop assistant looks startled at the hurricane that has just descended on this usually quiet and serene shop.

'So you gave the DVDs to us and now you want them back?' he asks.

'Yes, but I'll pay for them.'

'Is this what you're looking for?'

The old lady appears from nowhere, holding a Sainsbury's bag. Harry grabs it off her.

'Holy shit, you didn't die,' he tells her.

Harry lays the DVDs on the floor and counts them.

'They're all here. This is the greatest day of my life.'

'I thought one of the DVDs was sold?' I inquire, to both of the shop assistants.

'Don't worry, that DVD was already on display,' the old lady says.

'Why didn't you put my son's DVDs out?' I ask her.

'I felt bad for your boy, so I kept them around the back. I'm glad that I did.'

'So am I.'

What a kind gesture from a lovely lady, given that Harry hardly endeared himself to her. I take out a twenty-pound note and hand it to her.

'Thanks so much for doing that, please take this.'

She smiles and gratefully accepts the note.

An hour later we're back at the house. Harry is upstairs in his bedroom getting his Thomas fix, while I'm reading a newspaper, trying to unwind after another eventful day. The phone rings.

'David, it's Clarence here. Why the hell did you bring your son to the interview?'

'I had no choice. It was either that or cancelling it. What was their reaction?'

'Human Resources just rang. They commented on how well you interviewed before your son interrupted everything. I'm an astute guy, and reading between the lines I got the impression that your situation at home wouldn't have helped your case, given that this is a highly pressured job. Of course they didn't actually say that, but I'm pretty damn good at picking up signals. Next time please ring me and I'll arrange a babysitter, I know that's not in my job description, but hey, if it gets my client a job I'm willing to pull out all the stops for you.'

'It's not as simple as that, my son is autistic.'

'David, I'm extremely resourceful. I'll find someone.'

Clarence, you are full of shit.

'What exactly did your son say?' he asks.

I hesitate before I respond.

'He told Emma that she had big breasts and asked what shop she brought them from.'

'Oh my God, that's unbelievable,' Clarence replies, before cracking up. I can hear him relaying this story on to his colleagues and more laughter ensues.

'Clarence, are you still there?'

A minute later he gets back on the phone.

'Yeah, man, I'm here. That's the funniest thing I've ever heard, but it cost you the job. However, don't worry, my friend, because you've got potential, and I can guarantee you'll be a success if you follow my guidelines. Do you hear what I'm saying?'

Unfortunately I do.

There used to be a police recruitment leaflet with the heading 'dull it isn't', although my mum misread as 'dull, isn't it?' My time off work has been far from dull. I need to get back to work for some relaxation.

I'm still feeling stressed out and exhausted from this morning's events. Maybe now is the perfect time to go for a run, to relieve some of this tension.

It must be over three years since I last went running and the fact that I eventually find my running shoes in the attic is testimony to this. Now dressed in my running gear I look more like Ken Dodd, rather than Mo Farah.

I tell Harry to put on his shorts and trainers.

'But it's only fifty-six degrees Fahrenheit,' he says.

'We're going for a run, so get ready.'

'A run? That's a load of shit.'

'You can put your iPod on during the run. What songs have you got on it?'

'Summer Holiday.'

'That's it?'

'Yeah, Cliff Richard is an amazing man. I love it when Ade Edmondson hit Cliff over the head with a mallet when he's singing Living Doll.'

Ten minutes later we arrive at our local park.

'Now, don't go running off on your own, just stick with me.'

'Is my heart going to be pounding?'

'Your heart will be fine.'

It's mine that I'm worried about.

Harry presses the play button on his iPod and shoots off, singing 'Summer Holiday' at the top of his voice.

He starts gesturing his hands wildly as if he's conducting an orchestra. Of course this brings some strange looks from passers-by.

Although Harry is now a couple of hundred yards ahead of me, I can still hear him singing Summer Holiday. My attempts to get closer to him are futile, so I eventually stop and shout after him to do the same. However, with Cliff blasting in his ears he doesn't hear me. I'm now beginning to panic as I'm losing sight of him. I struggle back to my car and speed up the road that is alongside the park. After a few minutes I still can't see him, so I go even faster and then the inevitable happens; a police car appears from nowhere and starts flashing at me to pull over. However, my first concern is finding Harry so I continue to drive on, until I finally spot him. I get out of the car and chase after my son. I'm getting closer, but so are the two policemen behind me. I'd like to say that this is like something out of a James Bond film, but in reality it's more like a Benny Hill sketch.

I eventually catch up with Harry and grab his shirt, which causes us both to fall onto the grass.

'Why didn't you stop running?' I ask.

'My legs were forcing me, but I think they've gone to sleep now.'

The agitated policemen soon join us.

'Before we take you to the station, can you explain why you didn't stop when we flashed our lights? And why are you chasing after this boy?' one of them asks.

'We're going to the police station? That's fantastic. Do Starsky and Hutch work there?' Harry enquires.

'Are you taking the piss?' the other policeman enquires.

'I want to go to the slammer tonight. Can you hand-cuff me please?' Harry asks, with his two arms in a handcuff position.

'Get up, you're both coming in.'

'Do you have Sky TV in all the cells?'

'Let me explain …' I add.

And so I did. After which they kindly let me off with a warning for my speeding, but did take Harry's disability into consideration.

The drive home was as slow and careful as possible. All the time I kept thinking that they were secretly watching me, but I'm sure that they had better things to do on a Thursday night in Streatham.

After dinner I pour myself a glass of whisky, which is normally reserved for special occasions, but I'm in desperate need of something that'll make me feel better about life and I'm hoping that the whisky will do this as quickly as possible.

Not the first time this week I reflect on my current situation. I'm still extremely nervous about finding another job and despite the redundancy payout I need to get one quickly. My health has deteriorated in the past year and every day with Harry is extremely stress-ful. I have to resolve his future, which in turn will help mine. I'm increasingly fed up of arguing the residential school issue with Laura, but this is my only salvation, as cruel as that sounds. Can Laura's breakdown also happen to me?

Harry walks into the living room.

'Ah, whisky, that's my favourite,' he announces.

'You're not having any.'

'But JR Ewing in *Dallas* pours himself a glass of whisky when he comes home from work, so why can't I?'

'You're too young.'

'Larry Hagman is dead, but they're still showing him drinking whisky.'

Another illogical Harry conversation has commenced. I'm not aware that he's now watching *Dallas*, but at least it's a break from the inane train talk. While I'm still thinking about Larry Hagman, Harry grabs my glass and gulps down the remaining whisky. He doesn't even wince when he swallows.

'It's better on the rocks.'

'OK, I'll remember that the next time, now go off to bed.'

I'm too tired to reprimand him.

Music can be a cure for stress and tonight there's only one artist who can bring me out of my depression; Frank Sinatra. I put on the 'Songs For Swinging Lovers' CD and immediately sing along to 'You Make Me Feel So Young'. However, the phone ringing interrupts the Sinatra/McCarthy duet.

'I've just had a phone call from the police to verify that you are David McCarthy, the father of my son. They told me that you lost Harry in Streatham Common. So when were you going to tell me about this?' Laura asks.

'I'm sorry, I simply forgot.'

'You forgot to tell Harry's mother that you both had an encounter with the police? I find that hard to believe.'

Actually so do I, but it's the truth.

'Laura, it's been a stressful day. One to block out of my memory.'

'Before you do can you please tell me what happened?'

I spend the next ten minutes recalling the ill-fated run, the car chase with the police and the near arrest.

'Can you make sure that you do twelve months of hard training before you take Harry out on a run again?'

'Yeah, OK.'

I'm not in the mood for one of Laura's lectures.

'How did the interview go?'

'A disaster. Harry made a couple of inappropriate remarks to the Project Manager, so she abandoned the interview.'

'What did he say?'

'He wanted to know which shop she brought her breasts from.'

'Oh no. Where the hell is he picking up that from?'

'Apparently Robert's mother has breast implants.'

Laura doesn't respond.

'I can't control what Robert says to Harry in the school playground,' I add.

'I know, I just find it so distressing.'

'It's what normal kids of his age talk about.'

Our conversation ends on a civil note, but prior to that it was yet another tense encounter with my ex-wife. Of course she's concerned about Harry and I should have told her about the park incident, but I went for that run with the best intentions. I didn't think that the jog would end with me talking to two policemen about how I lost my son and why I was doing fifty-five miles an hour in a forty miles per hour speed limit.

I pour myself another glass of whisky and turn Frank up a notch or two. Hopefully this combination will help me forget another stressful day.

Harry and Bernadette

I went to bed after finishing off my second whisky last night, so thankfully I didn't wake up with a hangover.

I forgot to ask Laura about Sean and his kids. I hope that it works out for her, but it's going to be difficult. There's nearly always baggage to be brought into a new middle-aged relationship; typically it's children and ex-partners to take into consideration, but when the child is autistic, it makes it more complicated. Is there a future Mrs McCarthy out there who will willingly take Harry on board? Subconsciously I wonder if that's one of the reasons why I have stayed clear of a relationship.

I've been looking forward to today for a while, as it's Harry's concert rehearsal at his school. I still don't know which song they'll be singing, as whenever I ask Harry, he shrugs his shoulders. We're meeting at the school at ten, so hopefully all will be revealed then. I still can't believe that in two days' time Harry will be singing at the Royal Festival Hall. Unlike his father, Harry has a lovely voice, but apart from singing Thomas, Abba and Cliff Richard songs, he shows little interest in pursuing his talent. On my last birthday before Harry was born I went to a karaoke bar with Laura and a few friends and after a few pints I got up and sang 'Danny Boy' unaccompanied, as it wasn't available on the karaoke machine. All I can remember is a sea of bemused faces blankly staring at me and only a handful of people clapping afterwards. When I got back to my seat Laura told me that my voice was shit and warned me never to do that again in public.

Harry has also been playing the piano at school for the past year, but I'm ashamed to admit that I still haven't heard him play. I did offer to buy him a piano keyboard a couple of months ago, but he declined my offer, instead suggesting that I get him eleven DVDs.

Laura has the day off work, and is coming along too. She's equally excited at the prospect at seeing Harry at the Royal Festival Hall. Hopefully the occasion will override any lingering bad feelings between us after our telephone conversation yesterday. It'll be nice to share a happy time together for a change.

Probably our happiest period as parents was Harry's first year. He was an adorable baby, although even back then sleeping wasn't too high on his agenda. Strangers would stop us in the street and comment how lovely he was, which of course made us feel extremely proud. We went to Ireland when he was six months old to visit my million or so relatives, and only the Pope's visit drew more excitement. Everyone kept asking how many more children we planned on having, and our standard reply was always one or two. However, when Harry's problems started to become apparent we decided that one was enough.

Harry is sitting opposite me reading the Streatham telephone directory.

'What are you looking for?' I ask.

'You know; people.'

'Anyone in particular?'

'Just people, they're all in here,' Harry says.

'Are you looking forward to the concert rehearsal at the school?'

'I don't know why we're going; it's not a school day.'

'It's because the concert is on Saturday and you've got to practise the song.'

'But I've sang that pathetic song fifty-one times now, it's ridiculous,' Harry says, before resuming his telephone directory name check.

After our short conversation my thoughts turn to Mum. I haven't heard from her recently, so she's probably still annoyed after her last visit. It'll be up to me, as usual, to make the first move and contact her, although I'll avoid inviting her over again. Our last two encounters have proved extremely tense.

A couple of hours later I park my car outside the school.

'It's not fair that I have to go to school when I'm on holiday,' Harry moans.

'How many times do I have to explain this? You're not going for lessons, just rehearsing the song, that's all.'

'But we're still going *into* the school.'

'OK, Harry, let's drop it.'

We're met outside the school by Edward, Harry's music teacher.

'Thanks for dropping Harry off, it'll be over by twelve and then we're having some refreshments in the hall, so please come along to that,' Edward says.

'I was hoping to watch the rehearsals,' I add.

'That'll be too distracting for the children. Besides, you'll get to see the polished version on Saturday.'

'What song are they performing?'

I'm embarrassed to ask this question, as any decent parent who takes an interest in his child's school activities will already know the answer.

'I can't answer that. We've gone to great pains to keep it a secret until Saturday, when all will be revealed. Let's just say that you're in for a pleasant surprise.'

I'm mystified at the cloak and dagger approach. I'm sure that Harry would divulge the answer if I promise him a DVD, but I can wait.

Just as I'm leaving the school, Laura arrives.

'Has it started yet?' she asks.

'Shortly, but we're banned.'

'What do you mean?'

'Edward wants the rehearsals behind closed doors.'

'You're joking?'

'Afraid not. They must've found Elvis working at the Sainsbury's checkout in Brixton and he's in there with McCartney.'

'With Keith Moon on drums and Jimi Hendrix on guitar?' Laura asks.

'Now I'll pay money to see that group.'

'I'm so disappointed. I took the day off for this.'

'Do you fancy a coffee?' I ask.

'Yeah, why not.'

A few minutes later we're sipping our cappuccinos in a nearby Starbucks.

'Laura, I want to discuss Harry's future, but this time let's both try to remain calm and think about what's best for him.'

'You want to talk about his schooling?' Laura asks, sounding weary.

'Yes, but every time I bring this subject up it immediately causes an argument.'

'And I thought that this was going to be a fun day.'

'There you go again. You can't keep burying your head in the sand. Harry's needs are complex and he's extremely demanding. You get him once a week, but I'm with him the rest of time. I get no respite. You, of all people, must realise what a strain he can be.'

'So what do you suggest?' Laura enquires.

'Last week I contacted an autistic residential school called Star House, it's in Ipswich ...'

'Ipswich? You're joking, right?'

'I couldn't find any appropriate schools in London, so I contacted Star House last week. They told me if we wanted a look around the school, just ring the day before. They were extremely helpful.'

Laura appears tense, but at least she's not dismissing the idea.

'You have tomorrow off as well, don't you?' I ask.

'Yeah, I wanted to have a long weekend.'

'Shall I contact Star House and arrange for the three of us to go up there tomorrow?'

'You seem to have this all planned out.'

'No, I just thought about it this morning.'

That's a lie. I knew that Laura had tomorrow off and that I could get an appointment at the school. The only uncertainty is whether Laura is willing to make the trip.

'As the three of us are available, it's the perfect opportunity. Star House take a later summer break, so we'll be able to sit in on some of the lessons. I promise you, if you don't like it I won't pursue anything. There's nothing wrong in window shopping, is there?'

Laura takes another sip of her cappuccino, while staring at the delights of Streatham High Street. Two minutes of strained silence follows before she speaks.

'OK, let's do it.'

I'm surprised at her willingness to go along, I anticipated more of a fight.

'Can I ask why you have agreed this time?'

'There's no harm in having a look around the school, but don't get too excited just yet.'

I'll quit while I'm ahead. I don't want to spoil the present mood by talking about such a delicate and emotional topic.

'How's Sean?'

Her concerned expression changes to a smile at the mere mention of his name.

'He's good; things are going well between us.'

'And the kids?'

'Now that's another matter. They're still pissed off at Sean's punishment.'

'Did they ever apologise to you?'

'No. I don't know if they regret what they did; they don't give too much away.'

'How are they with you?'

'They're fine; no problem really.'

'So there's hope yet.'

Laura grins at my positive remark.

'And what about you? Have you seen Kerry lately?' Laura asks.

'Not for a couple of days, and before you start, there's nothing going on between us.'

'I'm not sure; she seems to like you.'

'We've as much chance of getting together as Spurs have of winning the premiership this season,' I add.

'When was the last time Arsenal won the premiership?'

Damn, she knows more than I expected. I can't even win a football argument against her.

'Anyway, I'm pleased that you've found someone. After all you've been through, you deserve some happiness,' I tell her.

'Thanks, but don't think I haven't noticed how you deftly changed the subject there.'

'I meant what I said.'

Once again, I think back to the most stressful time of all; Laura's breakdown. Harry's strange behaviour and his constant lack of sleep made Laura irritable for months. On one occasion she threw the remote control at me when I forgot to record *Coronation Street*. This resulted in a black eye for a month. To protect Laura, I told people that it happened while I was playing football. She was so apologetic afterwards, but the next confrontation wasn't far away. The doctor prescribed anti-depressant drugs, but after taking these for a while she simply didn't care about anything; me and Harry included. It was heartbreaking to watch and I'll never know what affect this had on Harry. My mother, in her subtle way, kept telling her to stop cracking up and pull herself together. It took two years for Laura to get better, but to her credit she did. However, our relationship never recovered.

After our cappuccinos, we spend the next couple of hours shopping. The subject of the residential school didn't crop up again.

We arrive at the school just as the children were coming out. Edward and Harry approach us.

'Harry was exceptional, weren't you?' Edward says, as he looks down at my son.

'It sounded crap,' Harry says.

'He's such a modest boy,' I interrupt.

'Harry's a wonderful piano player. Have you got a piano at home? It'll help if he could practise more often.'

'We're looking into it,' I vaguely respond.

'How many singers will be there on Saturday?' I ask.

'There'll be only six of us. Anyway I must dash. I'll see you all on Saturday and please don't forget to drop him off at five-thirty at the Festival Hall. I can't believe we're going to be on the same stage that my favourite singer of all time once performed.'

'Who's that?'

'Liza Minnelli.'

'Don't tell me that we're going to sing that shit song *again*?' Harry asks.

'Harry, please mind your language,' Laura tells him.

'It'll be the last practise session. We want to achieve perfection on Saturday,' Edward tells Harry.

'Can I bring my portable DVD player on stage, while those other idiots are singing?' Harry asks Edward, referring to the other main stream school, who will also be performing.

'Most definitely not. You'll be quiet and listen carefully to the wonderful music, I'm sure that you're going to love it,' Edwards sternly informs my son.

'How many light bulbs will there be on the stage? I don't like it too bright,' Harry enquires.

'That's enough, Harry. Edward has to go now,' I tell my son.

'Don't be late, remember every second counts in our strive for perfection,' Edward announces before departing.

I'm now beginning to realise why Harry hates music lessons so much.

As we're walking back to the car my mobile rings; it's Alice.

'David, I know that it's late notice, but can Harry come to the cinema tonight with Bernadette? That *Powerpuff* film is on at six o'clock at the Odeon. I don't mind picking him up and taking him if you're busy.'

'No, that'll be fine. I'll pop over to you at five-thirty and I'll take them to the cinema.'

'Are you sure?'

'Of course.'

'That's great, I'll see you then,' Alice says, before hanging up.

'Who was that?' Laura asks.

'Alice; Bernadette's mum. Bernadette and Harry are going to see that *Powerpuff* film and I'm going to be their chaperone,' I announce.

'What, you mean like a date?'

'Yeah, exciting isn't it?'

Although Bernadette asked Harry a couple of days ago, I forgot to mention this to Laura. But I won't confess; why spoil the moment?

'That's lovely,' Laura says, her lips slightly quivering.

'Harry, we're going to see the *Powerpuff* film tonight with Bernadette.'

'I hope they kick the shit out of the evil bastards.'

Laura and I smile at each other, and for once, neither of us reprimand him. I can tell that Laura is feeling immensely proud of her boy, who, for the moment, seems more interested in who the Powerpuff girls are going to beat up, rather than preparing for his first 'date'.

An hour later I'm at home drinking a cup of tea. I'm reflecting on the lovely stress-free morning that I shared with Laura. I still can't understand why she agreed so easily to the Ipswich trip, after so strongly opposing the idea previously. At the very least it'll be good to spend the day as a family; something we haven't done for a while.

Harry walks into the room.

'I like tying shoelaces; can I tie yours?' he asks.

'Yeah, if you like, but they are already tied.'

'They look like lumps of shit,' Harry observes.

Charming.

He bends down, unties my laces and then methodically ties them back again. This process takes nearly five minutes.

'That's better,' Harry remarks, after he completed his task.

'Thanks.'

'Maybe I can get a job tying laces?' my son enquires.

'I'm not sure there's a market for that.'

'I'm going to ask the manager of WH Smiths if I could get a Saturday job doing that. When the people come into the shop I'll show them my shoe laces and then do theirs for five pounds.'

'That's a bit steep, and I don't think WH Smiths have that job going right now.'

A disappointed Harry leaves the kitchen.

Harry's future job prospects are often on my mind. I know that he's only twelve years old and I do feel reassured that he'll get a job after my chat with the manager at the local supermarket, but I still worry. What skills will he learn at his school that will enable him to land a semi-decent job? Maybe Harry's shoe lacing idea will be the new craze when he leaves school and he'll end up a self-employed business entrepreneur?

I iron Harry's best pair of jeans and his light blue Calvin Klein shirt. I want him to look at his best tonight. Although Harry seems to be looking forward to the film, he doesn't appear to be over excited about seeing Bernadette.

I'll never forget my first date with Laura. We went to the cinema to see *It's a Wonderful Life*, which has always been my favourite film. She cried at the end and was subsequently embarrassed, which endeared her even more to me. We then went to an Italian restaurant and talked until one in the morning. I was ecstatic when she rang the next day to say that she wanted to meet up again. I feel both happy and sad when I recall that unforgettable night.

We're only a couple of minutes away from Bernadette's when Kerry rings me. I park the car, before ringing her back.

'David, I'm glad I caught you. Can you come over for dinner tomorrow night?'

'Yes, I think so. What's the occasion?'

'You've been so good looking after Niall this week, I'd like to show my appreciation.'

'There's no need.'

'A good deed shouldn't go unrecognised.'

I can't argue with that. We arrange to see Kerry tomorrow at six. It looks like it'll be another full day.

Looking after Niall twice this week has proved traumatic, but it's opened my eyes to life with a severely autistic child. I worry about Harry's future, but what of Niall? He has zero chance of ever securing a job, or even be in a relationship. I've no doubt that he'll have to go to a residential school within two to three years. How will Kerry cope with Niall when he gets older?

Ten minutes later I'm sitting in Alice's kitchen, waiting for Bernadette. I glance at my watch, it's now five forty-three and the film starts at six. Harry is pacing up and down, looking at the kitchen clock every few seconds.

'We're going to be late,' he informs me.

'No, we're not. It's only a five-minute walk from here.'

'But it's going to take nine minutes to queue up,' he says before dashing out into the hallway.

'Come on, get the fuck down here *now*,' he screams up the stairs.

'Harry, don't be so rude,' I tell my son.

He reluctantly returns to the kitchen.

At five forty-nine Alice and Bernadette come downstairs. Bernadette looks lovely in her pink dress, but Harry couldn't care less, as he rushes out of the front door without even acknowledging her.

'I'm sorry about that,' I say to Alice.

'No problem, it's our fault for running late.'

'Bernadette, you look so pretty. It was worth the wait,' I tell her.

'I wanted Mum to make me look like a whore; well do I?' Bernadette asks.

'No, you most certainly don't.'

We manage to catch up with Harry and arrive at the cinema at five fifty-six. However, it takes six minutes to purchase the tickets. It's worrying how I'm also getting obsessed about time-keeping.

'Do you want some popcorn?' I ask Harry and Bernadette.

'I don't like eating popcorn unless we're watching a film,' Harry responds.

'But we're going in shortly.'

'Can't you see it's now two minutes past six? The cinema is finished.'

'The actual film doesn't start until six-fifteen,' I try to explain.

'We're missing the adverts and the future films, so it's a waste of time.'

I look over at Bernadette, who nods in agreement.

'We can go tomorrow or Saturday,' she says.

We have plans for both of those days, but I don't tell her this. Oh well, that's twenty-eight pounds and fifty pence down the drain.

'What do you want to do now?' I ask them.

'I want to look at the tramps on Streatham Common drinking their beer,' Bernadette proclaims.

'You mean the homeless people?'

'I love those smelly shits, because they hate having baths.'

'We'll give that a miss today.'

Bernadette looks despondent. There must be better ways of killing a few hours on a summer's evening?

'Any other ideas?' I ask Harry.

'We should have left the house at five thirty-four.'

'Can we go to see *Mamma Mia*?' Bernadette asks.

'No, sorry.'

That's an improvement on hanging out with the homeless, but it'll be a while before I set foot inside that theatre again; especially with Harry and Bernadette.

'You know the rules, Daddy, why did you break the rules?' Harry questions.

'I don't know what you're talking about.'

'We should always arrive at the cinema twenty-one minutes before the film starts. We need nine minutes queuing-up time for the tickets, seven minutes for the lemonade and popcorn and five more minutes to get to our seats. Why did you cock it up?'

'That's enough now, Harry, let's drop it.'

Bernadette took a long time getting ready, and that's the reason we're late. However, I'm relieved that he's taking his anger out on me instead of her.

'So where do you want to go?' I ask again.

'Can we stay here for two hours? I want to look at the screen that show the film times,' Bernadette enquiries.

How can I turn her down again?

'Harry, does that sound OK?' I ask.

'Yeah, that's an amazing idea, but no popcorn.'

There's a small eating area next to the screen that displays all the twelve film times, so we settle to the nearest vantage point.

An hour later we're still monitoring the screen, which has now changed four times, when a film completes, it is removed from the screen. This is hardly the most exciting hour of my life, but as long as it keeps Harry and Bernadette happy.

'What the hell's the name of that film on screen eleven?' Bernadette asks.

'*Casablanca*,' I reply.

'Yeah, that's bollocks. Everyone in it is dead now,' Harry adds.

'Harry, it may be old, but it's still a great film,' I explain.

'There's no swearing, no sex and it's all in black and grey, which is stupid.'

'How come you know so much about this film?' I ask.

'Mummy has it on DVD and she played it on the nineteenth of July two thousand and thirteen. I was bored for one hundred and two minutes. It was shit and everyone kept smoking in it.'

I wonder if Harry could get a job on the BBC as an alternative film critic?

'Shall we leave now?' I ask.

'Are you kidding me? There is only twelve minutes before *Minions* finishes,' Bernadette says, looking at me as if I've lost my mind.

I knew that I should have bought my camcorder to record this momentous event.

'Have you got Thomas's autograph?' Harry asks Bernadette.

'No.'

'Me neither. What about Percy's?'

'No.'

'Edward?'

'No.'

'Maisie?'

'No.'

'Have you got any of the train's autographs?' I ask Bernadette, attempting to shorten the Q and A session.

'No.'

I'm not quite sure how any of the trains can actually write their autographs, but that question can wait until I've finally lost the will to live.

My only encounter with a celebrity, while with Harry, was when I spotted Jools Holland at Heathrow airport. The only 'celebrities' that I wouldn't seek an autograph from are television newsreaders and weather forecasters, so I approached Jools, carrying Harry's *Thomas the Tank Engine* magazine, as it was the only paper to hand, and asked for his autograph. At this point Harry tore open a packet of Skittles, causing them to fall onto the floor, by Jools's feet. Harry knelt down and started to pick them up and he literally punched Jools's ankle, telling him to 'move his fucking leg'. I then explained Harry's autism and he was really cool about it and even asked about his education. As we were walking away Harry shouted after him 'Don't you *ever* tread on my skittles again'. Jools gently smiled back, although he looked bemused.

'Mister McCarthy, why aren't there any pink dogs?'

'I'm not sure …'

'Did England invent the cat?' she asks.

'No.'

'Where were they invented then?'

'Cats have been around forever.'

'Mister McCarthy, are you a simpleton?'

I'm impressed that she knows what simpleton means, even though she's associating the word with me.

'I don't think so,' I reply.

'Harry, is your dad a simpleton?'

'You mean like Forest Gump?'

Again I'm impressed.

'Yeah, that's who he reminds me of,' Bernadette agrees.

'Daddy is only a little bit like Forest Gump.'

I suppose I should be grateful for that.

This evening hasn't panned out quite as I thought, but it's lovely to see Harry and Bernadette enjoying themselves and interacting with each other, albeit at my expense.

'Do you like Bernadette's pink dress?' I ask my son.

Harry continues to stare at the screen.

'Harry, look at me,' I say more firmly, my face only a couple of inches from his, leaving him with little option but to acknowledge me.

'Do you like Bernadette's dress?'

He seems confused, and still doesn't respond, so I don't pursue it.

A few minutes later Harry and Bernadette cheer loudly, as they greet the disappearance of *Minions* on the screen. Several people look over at us, and then glance up at the screen, to see what caused such a reaction and bemused expressions follow as they all can observe is a boring screen showing film screen times and nothing else.

A short time later I tell Harry and Bernadette it's time to leave. One hour and thirty-seven minutes looking at that screen has fried my brain. Although they don't complain, Harry and Bernadette continue to stare at the screen, even when we're outside the cinema.

'Did you enjoy yourself tonight?' I ask my passengers on the car journey back to Bernadette's house.

'It was wild,' Bernadette responds.

Wild isn't quite the word I would use; tedious and monotonous are more accurate.

'Yeah, it was awesome; can we do it again soon?' Harry asks.

'We'll see, ' I cautiously reply.

'Can we go to the *Powerpuff* film tomorrow night? But this time make sure that you don't piss around,' Harry firmly tells me.

'We're going to Niall's for dinner tomorrow night.'

'But he doesn't speak.'

'I'm aware of that.'

'Doesn't he want to talk to anyone?' Harry asks.

'Yes, he does, but he can't.'

'He better not make too much noise, it drives me crazy,' Harry says, putting his hands over his ears.

'That's the only way that Niall can communicate and if you're rude to him you'll find that your Thomas DVDs will go missing.'

'Not again,' Harry moans.

Although Harry is extremely vocal, he's intolerant of the more severely autistic child, who usually only vocalises by making grunting noises. A lot of autistic children are particularly sensitive to noise, but I will not tolerate my son discriminating against another autistic child.

As I'm parking the car in Alice's driveway, she comes out to greet us.

'Did you enjoy the film?' she asks her daughter.

'We never saw it, because of Dad,' Harry interrupts.

Alice looks up at me.

'We were a few minutes late for the adverts and trailers, and that was unacceptable,' I explain.

'Did you see another film?'

'No, we watched the screen that shows the film times for one hour and thirty-seven minutes,' Bernadette adds.

'Are you in need of a beer?' a smiling Alice asks me.

'Several, actually.'

An hour later Alice and I are sitting in her livingroom, whilst the kids are upstairs.

'So, where's Francis?'

'He's in Brussels on business, and won't be back until Monday.'

'Is he away a lot?'

'Not enough,' Alice snaps, while staring at her wine glass.

'I'm sorry, I didn't mean to intrude.'

'There's no need to apologise. We're going through a rough spell at the moment, as Bernadette inadvertently let slip the other day.'

I am surprised at her openness.

'Fatherhood is never the top of his priorities I'm afraid,' she adds.

My first encounter with Alice was strained. Initially I thought that she was snooty, but after spending some time with her I now realise that this isn't true. She's a lovely and caring person and it seems that she's not getting too much help in bringing up Bernadette. Although it's different circumstances to Danny, both of the fathers are selfishly neglecting their children, which from my experience in the autistic world is all too common.

'I admire you for bringing up Harry on your own,' Alice tells me.

'Because of Laura's illness I've had no choice.'

'Still, it must be difficult for you.'

I shrug my shoulders, feeling embarrassed.

'I better be going now. Thanks again for the drink.'

'One more for the road?'

'I'd love to, but that would put me over the limit.'

'Of course; very sensible.'

Soon afterwards Harry joins me in the hallway.

'This house is the dog's bollocks,' he enthusiastically announces.

'Harry, please stop the swearing.'

'What do you like about the house?' Alice enquires.

'Sky TV, the toilet seat and the blue carpet on the stairs.'

In that order I presume.

'Did you enjoy your night out with Bernadette?' Alice asks.

'Oh yeah, Bernadette is now number three of my top eleven friends.'

Alice and I look proudly at each other.

'What's your middle name?' Harry asks Bernadette.

'Susan.'

'Oh; you're now my number four friend.'

Bernadette nods, as if she understands my son's logic.

I'm happy knowing that Bernadette is still in the prestigious top five.

'Thanks so much for taking the kids tonight. As I now have your mobile, there's no need for me to ring the Odeon for the showing times,' Alice jokingly says as we're leaving.

'No problem. I'm glad it was a success.'

On the car journey home I reflect on today. It started off with the disappointment of not seeing Harry's rehearsal, but that led to spending some quality time with Laura. Despite Harry's annoyance at missing out on the film, watching the film times on the screen proved exciting for Harry and Bernadette, although less so for me. I wish that Laura could have seen the way the kids interacted with each other. If there's another opportunity and Alice can't make it, I'll ask Laura to go in place of me.

As I'm lying alongside Harry in bed, instead of pondering on the stressful events of the day, or the prospect of being made redundant, or my recent health scare, I think positively on the wonderful evening that I've just shared with my boy and his lovely, fourth best friend.

Star House

'Ipswich is ninety-three miles from London. Don't forget to drive along the A214, then the A23, A236, A212, A2022, A232, A21, M25, A12, A1214, A1071 and the last road is the A1022. It'll take you two hours and twelve minutes. You've done three minutes and twenty-eight seconds so far,' Harry tells me as he looks at his stopwatch. I told Harry last night that we were going to look at a school in Ipswich. He immediately googled Ipswich, but did not ask me why we were looking at the school.

'If we went by train it would've only taken us only one hour and seven minutes. The train leaves from Liverpool Street station and costs thirty-nine pounds and eighty pence return. Haven't you thirty-nine pounds and eighty pence, Daddy?'

'Yes, he has, but we wanted to go by car. I think that we've covered all the journey options now,' Laura remarks.

'We could've gone from Victoria coach station, which arrives at Ipswich rail station in three hours and fifty minutes. That would've cost twenty-two pounds return.'

'Are there any other ways of getting to Ipswich?' Laura asks her son.

'Ipswich is a bit shit. All it has is boring churches.'

'Harry, that's disrespectful. Don't you know that the church is the house of God?'

'Is it? I've never seen him. He isn't that weird bloke who wears a dress and talks all the time about Mary and keeps on saying Amen again and again and again?'

I immediately park the car.

'Don't you *ever* talk about God and the church like that again,' I shout at Harry.

He's still looking at his stopwatch.

Do I make myself clear?'

'But why don't the people in the church ever laugh?' Harry asks.

'You go to the church to pray to God, not to have a laugh,' I explain.

There have been a number of occasions when Harry would burst into laughter during the Mass, for no explicable reason. The parishioner's Christian attitude was severely tested during these hysteria outbursts. After the first such eruption I spoke to the priest, to explain Harry's autism. He was extremely understanding and assured me that it had the positive affect of waking up the rest of the congregation.

But worse was still to come. A couple of years ago when Harry was at the altar to receive his First Holy Communion, he kicked the priest in his shin. When the priest was bent over in agony I swear I heard him say 'Oh fu...', but managed to stop himself just in time. The congregation gasped at Harry's attack, most of whom are unaware of Harry's autism. Once again the priest graciously dismissed the incident, but I did notice that he walked with a limp for a couple of weeks afterwards.

It seems that Harry and I are now the local church celebrities. If there was a church ASBO, then Harry would be the first recipient.

Coming from an Irish background, Catholicism ruled in our household. We attended Mass at least once a week and regularly went to Confession. I remember staying up to watch the Irish comedian Dave Allen on TV, but we were only allowed to watch it up to the point when the inevitable religious joke or sketch came on and the TV would then be switched off. It was the only time that I heard my dad swear.

Although I don't have the level of faith that my parents had, I still go to church every Sunday, even though it's probably the most stressful hour of the week.

'Shall we tell him the purpose of our trip?' Laura quietly asks me.

'I'm not sure.'

'If he goes to this school, Harry will be allowed to come back at the weekends, right?'

'It's up to us, but he can stay all week.'

'He'll never tolerate that.'

I can feel a tense atmosphere already. How committed is Laura? Maybe she's coming along just to pacify me? I'm also having my own doubts. It would break my heart to send my boy away to a residential school. I've no idea how he'll cope. I feel sick at the thought of making this decision, but I've got to think about what's best for everyone, including Harry.

'How's Sean?' I enquire, changing the subject.

Laura looks at me, but doesn't respond.

'Is anything wrong?' I ask.

'Sean wants me to move in with him.'

'Wow, that was quick. Are you going to?' I ask, looking at my rear view mirror to see if Harry is paying attention to our conversation, but his head is buried in the Streatham telephone directory. A fine read.

'I don't know. Maybe it's too soon. And of course there's Harry to take into consideration. What happens when he stays overnight or even for a few hours? The last encounter with Timothy and Mary doesn't exactly fill me with confidence,' Laura says.

'If you move in with Sean, you'll know after a few weeks if it's working out.'

'So you're advising me to move in?'

'No, that's your decision.'

'Mum, are you moving out of that shithole?' Harry asks.

I didn't think that Harry was paying attention.

'I don't know.'

'Has that bloke with the funny voice got Sky TV?'

'Yes, Sean has Sky.'

'Then you *have* to live with him, so I can come and visit you.'

'That's two positive votes, although I'm not certain that Harry has my best interests at heart,' Laura smiles.

Does that look indicate that a decision has just been made or simply relief that she has unburdened her dilemma?

I'm trying to act positively for Laura, but I'm stunned at this development. After all, it was only three days ago when I first found out that she was dating.

'Thanks for your support, David; that means a lot.'

The moving in with Sean subject is not brought up again as Frank Sinatra, Simon and Garfunkel and The Beatles accompany us all the way to Ipswich.

'Two hours, twenty-six minutes and fifty-three seconds. What went wrong, Daddy?' Harry asks, upon our arrival at the school.

'I took a couple of wrong side roads in Ipswich,' I tell him.

Why do I have to account for the extra fourteen minutes and fifty-three seconds to my son?

'That's ridiculous.'

'Come on, let's get going,' I say.

We're met at the school by Ella, who is one of the teachers.

'So this is Harry,' she says enthusiastically.

'Who the hell are you?' Harry abruptly asks.

'I'm Ella; I teach here.'

'Why are we at this dump?'

'Harry's annoyed because we arrived late,' I add.

'You made pretty good time. It's a long way from London,' Ella tells Harry.

'It's ninety-three miles and we should've completed it in two hours and twelve minutes. It said so on the AA route planner, but Daddy was pissing around. He kept going up and down the same fucking street again and again.'

This isn't the first impression that I was hoping for.

OK, Harry, that's enough swearing,' Laura tells her son.

'I'm sorry about that,' I say to Ella.

'Please, there's no reason to apologise. I understand,' Ella replies in a confident and calm manner.

Ella then takes us straight into a class. We sit at the back, observing the lesson. The class are eleven to twelve year olds, which is Harry's peer group.

After a few minutes one of the pupils approaches us.

'What time did you have a shave this morning?' he asks me, while intensely studying my face.

'Er … about six o'clock, I think.'

He runs his fingers alongside both of my cheeks.

'Pretty smooth, what razor did you use?'

'BICS,' I reply.

'That must have been the first or second shave, using that razor?'

'Yes, it was brand new.'

He smiles before smelling my cheeks.

'Why didn't you put any aftershave on?' the boy enquiries.

'OK, Richard, can you rejoin the class now please?' his teacher asks.

Richard returns to his seat, but remains focused on me, presumably awaiting my response.

'I forgot,' I mutter.

The rest of the class are now looking at me.

'It's pointless having a shave, unless you put on after-shave when you're finished. Don't forget in the future, OK?' an agitated Richard informs me.

I nod my response.

'OK, class, can you resume our lesson?'

'I recommend the Polo aftershave, you can get it in Boots for nineteen pounds and ninety-nine pence.'

'The lesson today is about the correct social behaviour when in a restaurant,' the teacher says.

Most 'normal' twelve-year-olds will know the do's and don'ts when in this type of situation (whether they abide by them is another matter), but twelve-year-old autistic children have to be constantly taught this behaviour.

'First of all, when you give your order to the waitress, always say please at the end.'

'What's the point of that?' one of the pupils asks.

'Because it's important to be polite.'

'I am only polite *after* I've had my dinner.'

'No, that's not the way it works. You say can I have my chips *please*? And when the waitress gives them to you, you say *thank you*.'

'I always tell them to hurry up with my food.'

That sounds familiar. I'm reassured that Harry isn't the only person on this earth who makes such comments.

Harry quickly strides to the front of the classroom and stands there staring at the teacher.

'Hello, can I help you?' the teacher asks.

'You're ugly.'

I immediately dash towards him.

'Harry, get back here now.'

But my son continues to stare at the teacher.

'Why do you say that?' the teacher enquires, seemingly unfazed by my son's outburst.

'You've got a big, stupid wart on your face, you're fat and your mad hair makes you look like a scarecrow.'

'I'm really sorry about this,' I say to the teacher, 'come on, Harry we've got to go.'

'No, it's OK, let me talk this through with him,' the teacher responds, although I notice there is more of an edge to her voice.

'Did you understand what I was just saying about being polite?' she asks Harry.

'No.'

'Let me explain then. Being polite means that you're being nice to people and the opposite of being polite is?'

Harry simply shrugs his shoulders.

'It means being rude and that's what you did to me just now. Do you see what I'm saying?'

'I wasn't being rude, I was just telling the truth.'

I gently take Harry's hand and steer him away from the teacher, who now looks upset. I know that if she continues to pursue this line of questioning, she'll only feel worse.

'Miss, that boy is right,' Richard shouts, 'you *do* look hideous.'

There's no better time for us to leave. I take Harry out to the corridor and nervously await Laura and Ella. Oh well, this is one school we can now cross off our list.

'Shall we make our way back home? I think the guided tour has come to an abrupt end,' Laura says, as soon as she walks out of the classroom.

'Where's Ella?' I ask.

'She's talking to the teacher.'

'We should at least wait for her.'

'We're going now? But that was only a short time in Ipswich,' Harry says.

'Shut the fuck up,' I angrily respond.

My timing couldn't have been worse, as Ella is now standing just behind me.

'How is she?' Laura asks, nodding towards the classroom.

'She's OK, but personal insults, whether intentional or not, still hurt.'

That means that she's not OK.

'He doesn't understand that it's socially unacceptable to make such comments.'

I cannot believe that I'm defending him.

'I know and she's also aware of that. We've many programmes that deal with this type of inappropriate behaviour.'

'Thanks so much for your time,' I say, 'I'm sorry that we wasted it. We'll make our own way out.'

'Don't you want to see the rest of the school?'

'I thought that because of Harry's outburst …'

'That we wouldn't think of accepting Harry here?' Ella concludes my sentence.

'Well, yes.'

'We've plenty of Harry's. You just spoke to one of them; Richard. So shall we carry on?'

I smile and indicate her to lead the way.

'I'm sorry for swearing just then.'

'You seem to spending a lot of your time apologising. I've heard that word many times before, but rarely with as much passion,' Ella smiles.

I glance at Laura, who's shaking her head. That's not a good sign.

We are next shown the wonderful outdoor playing facilities in five acres of land, visit another classroom and talk to a couple more teachers. The atmosphere here is warm and friendly. I'm impressed.

Ella then shows us the overnight respite centre. Each student has its own bedroom, where they can hang their favourite posters on the wall. Wayne Rooney was in the first bedroom, while predictably, Thomas the Tank Engine was in the other three. The showers are situated just outside the bedrooms, where you can also have your own shower cubicle if you feel bashful, which in Harry's case is not relevant, as he tends to take all his clothes off at the drop of a hat.

There are also several televisions and computers to occupy the students. A series of daily chores, such as washing up, cooking, polishing the furniture, taking the rubbish out etc, is pinned up on the notice board, in addition to the student assigned to the task. Harry could be their toughest challenge yet on that one.

'I'd like to show you one more class before you go,' Ella tells us.

A couple of minutes later we take our now customary position at the back of the classroom. Eight pupils and four assistants are in this class, and it's clear to see why, as the pupils are severely autistic.

The assistant nearest to us has a board in front of the pupil with square, circle, diamond and rectangle shapes. The boy is holding a square object and attempting to associate it to the appropriate shape on the board. It's heartbreaking to watch him endeavour to manoeuvre the square object into the circle shape. The assistant is so patient and with the use of Makaton symbols manages to explain to the pupil the correct shaped object to pick up. She acts joyous when he finally completes his task, but the boy simply stares at the floor. She shows the boy the Makaton sign for good work.

Another student throws the object board against the wall in frustration and then repeatedly knees his forehead until the assistant stops him. My tight hamstrings would prevent me from doing this, even if I had the desire, but that boy has no such problems. The shuddering noise when the knee connects to the forehead is not for the faint-hearted.

Just as we're leaving, another pupil spits in an assistant's face. She calmly wipes it off with a tissue and continues with her task. My admiration for all the teachers of autistic children is immense, but they rarely get the recognition that they deserve. I despair when I hear of some Z list celebrity who gets an award in the Queen's honour list. Maybe the Queen should spend a day at an autistic school, before deciding the recipients of these awards.

The last few minutes have been a humbling experience.

'Unlike a lot of other special needs schools, we have pupils at both ends of the autistic spectrum,' Ella tells us.

'Can any of those children speak?' Laura asks, nodding towards the classroom.

'Only one; Tommy, and his vocabulary extends to just yes and no.'

We chat for a few more minutes and Ella assures us that if we send in an application for a placement at the school it will be seriously considered, which is a relief after the 'ugly' incident. Harry, to his credit, has remained quiet since his outburst, but showed little interest in the class activities. How can anything that the school has to offer compete against the Streatham telephone directory?

'What did you think of the school?' I ask Harry, as we start our car journey home.

'Rubbish.'

'Why is it rubbish?'

'The classrooms are all painted white and there are no stairs.'

'What colour should the classrooms be?'

'Sky Blue.'

'Did you like Ella?'

'No, I don't like brown eyes and she smiles too much.'

'There must be something that you liked?' Laura asks Harry.

Harry ponders this question carefully before responding.

'The mirror in the toilet. It has a light above it.'

I wait for a few minutes, thinking that it's the ideal opportunity for Laura to voice her opinion, but she doesn't.

'So what do *you* think of the school?' I nervously ask her.

She hesitates before responding.

'I couldn't fault it. The lessons are well structured, the teachers are focused and the overnight facilities are second to none. Ella even managed to put a positive slant on Harry's customary outburst. What more can I say?'

Although I agree with Laura's comments, I'm surprised at her wholehearted endorsement for Star House.

'So you think that it's the right school for Harry?'

'If you're asking me should he go there at the earliest opportunity, then no, but it's an option to consider when the time is right.'

That was a less enthusiastic response.

'Believe it or not, David, I do understand the stress that you're under with Harry, after all, it nearly destroyed me. But don't you think that you should contact Social Services first and try again to arrange overnight respite for a couple of times a month and take it from there?'

This is the sensible approach. Only in exceptional circumstances will Harry be allowed to join Star House after the Christmas or Easter holidays, so the earliest that he'll be able to get into the school will probably be September of next year. I've tried, without success, to get him overnight respite in the past few months, but I'll now pursue this again. It'll give me a good indication on whether he's ready for Star House. I already feel a wonderful sense of relief, knowing that I can put off making the school decision for a few months.

'Laura, you're right; thanks.'

Laura notices my relaxed expression and smiles back at me.

'And I'm sorry for constantly doubting your motives. Coming here today has taught me not to be so narrow-minded and negative about other opportunities for Harry,' she concedes.

'Daddy, can we go to KFC in Streatham? I promise not to fart after eating the beautiful beans.'

How can I deny him the opportunity *not* to fart?

'Two hours, four minutes and fifty-two seconds was the journey from Ipswich to KFC,' Harry reminds me for the third time since our arrival at this salubrious restaurant.

'I'm so pleased that you've finally listened to me about how to drive properly,' he adds.

I notice that I have a voice message on my mobile: it's from Clarence.

'Hiya, my friend. I've come through for you again. I've set up an interview for next Friday at twelve. It's a consulting company called FasterTrack. They primarily work for a retail organisation, but I can't give too much away at this point, if you catch my drift.'

No, I haven't got a clue, mate.

'Anyway, give me a bell as soon as you can and I'll fill you in. I believe in you as a person, you have a great talent, so let's have a brain storming session next week to make sure that come next Friday you know exactly what colour underpants the CEO at FasterTrack wears and that we're singing from the same song sheet. You are the dog's bollocks of the computer program-ming world and don't you forget it. Stay chilled.'

I now have a moral dilemma; remain unemployed , resulting in financial ruin or secure a good paying job, but having to deal with Clarence in order to do so. A tough choice.

No seriously, I'm delighted that Clarence has set up the interview and Harry will be back in school by then so that isn't an issue.

'Is everything OK?' Laura anxiously enquires.

'Yeah, I've another interview for next week.'

'That's great, I'm so pleased for you.'

'Daddy, can you ask that man for an extra spoonful of beans please? There was seventeen spoons of beans last week and this week it's only fifteen. Has the bean man lost his mind?'

'Let's just throw caution to the wind and order another portion, shall we?' I respond.

'Two portions of beans? Wait until I tell Robert about this.'

'You might live to regret that decision,' Laura jokingly tells me.

'I'm having a few people over to the house before the concert tomorrow. Can you make it?' I ask.

'Why did you invite people around *before* the concert?'

'I originally invited Fiona and Isabelle and then Harry wanted Robert and Stephanie and so on. It'll take my mind off the concert. Don't worry, I'll tell them that they have to leave by four, so we can get ready. It'll be a fun pre-concert party.'

'There's a bit of Harry logic in there. I think you may be cramming too much in for one day, but what the hell. What food have you got?'

'I'm going to pop into Sainsbury's first thing in the morning and pick up loads of booze and snacks; it's no big deal.'

'I'll do some cooking tonight and bring it all over tomorrow.'

Half an hour later I drop Laura off at her flat.

'I'll see you tomorrow at around eleven,' Laura tells me as she opens the car door.

'OK, and thanks for being with me today; it was lovely.'

'Yeah; we had a good time.'

She leans over and kisses me on the cheek.

'Mummy, I want to go to that bloke's house on Sunday, because at ten past four *Ice Age Two* is on the Disney channel.'

'Haven't you got that on DVD?' Laura asks.

'Yes, but it's much better on the Disney channel.'

'We're all a bit busy tomorrow, but Sean may be coming around to the house before the concert, so you can ask him yourself.'

'OK, but when we go to his house he better not give me peas or that broccoli shit, or I'll throw them in his bath tub.'

I concur, as I don't want that habit making a comeback.

'I'll see you both tomorrow. I hope you have a nice time at Kerry's,' Laura says with a wry smile.

When I got home I spent the following hour on the phone inviting more people to the house before the concert tomorrow. To my surprise everyone can make it. I leave the most difficult call to last.

'Hello, Mum, how are things?'

'Oh, you've decided to speak to me, after being so abrupt the other day.'

'I'm not getting into that right now, I just want to know if you'll like to come over tomorrow before the concert. Say around twelve?'

'You're not seriously going to take that boy to the Royal Festival Hall, are you?'

'Yes, Mum, he's rehearsed his song many times, so it won't be a problem,' I say, sounding more confident than I feel.

'He'll start swearing and shouting on the stage and probably throw the instruments out into the audience. It'll be all over the newspapers and we'll be a laughing stock.'

How do I politely tell my mother that's she's losing the plot?

'No, he'll be fine,' I lie.

'Are you going to be on stage with him, so he doesn't get up to any mischief?'

'Mum, are you coming or not?' I ask, abruptly.

'I'm not sure.'

'OK, I hope to see you tomorrow,' I slam the phone down.

That conversation didn't exactly build any bridges.

I'm still angry as I park the car in Kerry's driveway. Why does my mum have to always be so negative about Harry? Doesn't she realise that he has a disability and cannot help some of his actions?

Harry is already knocking on Kerry's front door, before I'm even out of the car. It was nice of Kerry to invite us over, but it's been a long day and all I feel like doing right now is crashing out in front of the TV, with a can of beer.

Kerry walks out to greet me.

'Slight change of plan. I'm running late and have only just put the dinner on. While it's cooking do you fancy popping down to the pub for a couple? The Queen Vic is only a five minute walk from here.'

'That's a perfect idea.'

Ten minutes later we're sitting in the beer garden, enjoying our drinks on a beautiful summer's evening. The beer garden is crowded, which makes me nervous. Although we're situated at the far end of the garden, there are enough occupied tables nearby. Niall is sitting next to me and making loud grunting noises, which gets quizzical looks from a few people.

'He seems a bit anxious,' I say to Kerry.

'No more than usual.'

Niall is gritting his teeth and banging his Action Man on our wooden table.

'How are you today?' I ask him.

He doesn't acknowledge me, and stares blankly ahead.

I gently take his Action Man off him and pretend that it is shooting Harry. This doesn't please Niall as he takes it off me and proceeds to whack me across the face with it. The machine gun that the Action Man is holding catches me just above the eye and it immediately draws blood. It hurts like hell. The gash doesn't seem too severe, but an inch lower and I would have been in trouble.

I knew that this day was going too well.

Niall calmly walks away and simply stares at the clouds above him.

Kerry immediately gets up and approaches her son.

'What the hell did you do that for?' she shouts at her son.

We now have the attention of all the pub clientele.

'I'll be back in a few minutes,' I say, before heading towards the toilet to assess the damage. Everyone is looking at me as I have to walk through them in order to reach the pub.

'Why do you put up with that bullshit? There's no discipline today, and that's why these kids can get away with anything,' someone remarks.

I glance at the middle-aged man, but don't respond.

In the toilet I wipe the blood from my forehead and fix a plaster to it. It stings and is still hurting, but I'll survive.

'I'm so sorry, David, I feel terrible,' Kerry tells me upon my return.

'No problem. I shouldn't have taken his Action Man. It was pointless to attempt any imaginative play with him.'

Kerry nods.

'I didn't mean to sound that harsh,' I tell her.

'These random acts of violence frighten me.'

'Have you considered giving him Ritalin?' I ask.

'I've an appointment with his paediatrician on Wednesday; I'll discuss it with her then.'

I notice that some people are still looking at us. Normally this wouldn't bother me, but tonight it does.

Niall brings over the menu to me and points at the chips photo on it.

'When has he started doing this?' I ask Kerry.

'Only yesterday. I'm so excited that he's now trying to communicate at some level.'

He continues to point to the chips photo, but is looking increasingly agitated.

'Niall, no chips. We're going to have dinner soon,' Kerry tells him.

He grits his teeth again and hits his forehead with his fist. I'm on guard in anticipation of a further attack. A couple of minutes pass by and just as we're thinking that he's getting over his disappointment he dashes off to a nearby table, grabs a handful of chips off an elderly man and devours them. The man looks stunned, so Niall seizes the moment and takes a huge swill of his lager, but then immediately spits it out all over the man's shirt.

Harry wouldn't have been so wasteful.

Kerry and I arrive soon afterwards, as the man is wiping his shirt.

'I've *never* in my seventy-two years seen such disgraceful behaviour. I'm going straight to the manager to insist that you are barred. This is totally unacceptable,' he screams at us.

'If you're leaving now, can I have the rest of your chips?' Harry asks him.

Harry's timing is never good.

Before the man has a heart attack, I interrupt.

'Look, we're really sorry for all of this. These two boys are autistic and their behaviour can be unpredictable.'

'Unpredictable? Is that how you describe it? Whatever illness they have there's no excuse for their actions. I've heard enough.'

'Let me buy you another meal and have your shirt dry cleaned,' I say, taking out my wallet.

He storms off towards the pub, dismissing my suggestion with a wave of his hand. The rest of the clientele in the beer garden continue to stare.

I put a couple of twenty pound notes underneath the near empty beer glass.

'There's forty pounds here for the man, please do not nick it,' I shout at the onlookers.

'Come on, we're going,' I say to Kerry. 'I'm not hanging around for some for some officious pub manager to tell us where we can, or cannot, have a drink.'

I take Harry's hand and lead the way to the back entrance of the beer garden. Kerry and Niall are struggling to keep up.

I'm still fuming by the time we reach Kerry's house. I'm not stupid enough to realise that the man shouldn't have reacted to what happened, but to totally dismiss my autism explanation is hard to forgive. Thankfully this man's reaction is the exception.

Kerry opens her front door and it's only now when I notice the redness in her eyes.

When she gets into the kitchen she slumps into a chair, while Niall ventures out to the garden.

'I'll have to send him to residential school. I can't cope, and it's only going to get worse.'

'We went to Star House, in Ipswich today,' I say, although I'm not sure if my timing is right.

'How was it?' she asks, glancing up at me.

'Excellent, one definitely for the future.'

'Why not now?'

'We want him to get more overnight respite first and then take it from there.'

Kerry slowly gets up to check the state of the dinner.

'Another fifteen minutes,' she mutters.

I look over at Niall who is constantly spitting onto his fingers and carefully watching his saliva drop onto the patio. I've seen him do this a lot lately.

Kerry looks at me and then at Niall.

'That's another disgusting habit,' she remarks. 'It does tend to get a reaction when he performs that party trick in public.'

I feel partly to blame for the events of the past hour. Niall was a little edgy, but overall OK, until I took his Action Man off him. His mood changed dramatically after that.

While Kerry prepares the meal I stroll out to the garden.

In the distance I can hear a dog barking and Niall is looking in that direction, with a concerned expression. He relaxes when the barking stops.

Given what happened earlier I'm wary of approaching him. Although I'm only a couple of feet away from him, I might as well be invisible, as he doesn't even glance at me.

His concentration is intense, as he once again spits onto his hand and carefully watches the saliva trickle onto the ground. Once this task is complete, he starts his grunting noises again.

He strides around the garden with a purpose, almost as if he's late for an appointment. He's constantly flicking all his fingers in front of his eyes, which gets him excited and consequently noisier.

Niall is fascinating to watch.

He then sits down by the bushes and grabs a handful of dirt and immediately eats it. This pastime is shared by Harry. Niall and Harry obviously love dirt, personally I can't see the attraction and just hope that we're not having it for dinner.

I sit next to him, but he still doesn't acknowledge my existence.

He has a constant worried and sad expression, which troubles me. Does he know more than he lets on? We'll probably never know.

'Come on, dinner's ready,' Kerry shouts from the kitchen.

Niall jumps to his feet and runs towards the house. Like Harry, food is seemingly his top priority.

Four plates of shepherd's pie are already on the table by the time I arrive. Niall is frantically eating his dinner, as if he hadn't tasted food for weeks. He's constantly eyeing up everyone else's plates, ready to pounce given half a chance.

'Eat your own dinner, Niall, and don't go scrounging,' Kerry tells him.

'Yeah, if you lay your hands on my shepherd's pie I'll slit your throat,' Harry adds.

'Harry, that's enough of that kind of talk,' I admonish.

Niall glances into the kitchen to see if there's any shepherd's pie left on the stove, even though he isn't halfway through his own.

'I suppose we should be grateful that both the boys love their food. Some of them have some strange eating habits,' I say.

'You're right. There's a boy in Niall's class who only eats fish fingers for breakfast and dinner.'

'Must make the grocery shopping a bit easier though,' I remark, which Kerry responds to with a smile.

'Kerry, please don't make any rash decisions about what we talked about earlier. Talk it through with your paediatrician first. The correct medicine can make all the difference.'

Kerry half-heartedly nods.

'Niall's a bit of a lazy bastard,' Harry blurts out.

'What the hell are you talking about?' I ask.

'He can't be arsed to speak.'

'How many times must we go through this? You're one of the lucky ones because you can speak; Niall can't.'

'Why does he always making noises like a gorilla?'

227

'He doesn't, and stop being so insulting, OK?' I say.

Kerry doesn't appear to be too bothered by Harry's remarks, but she does seem to be in a world of her own right now.

Niall then starts tapping my plate with this fork.

'Does he want some of my food?' I ask Kerry.

'Yeah, but please don't feel obliged.'

As I am now scared of any repercussions, I hand him a generous portion, which he immediately tucks into, even though he still has plenty left of his own.

'What the hell's going on there?' Harry asks.

I hand over what's left of my plate to Harry. What I had of the shepherd's pie was delicious, but I need to eat faster.

Ten minutes later it's only Kerry and me at the table. Harry dashed upstairs, no doubt investigating Niall's DVD collection, whilst Niall is pacing up and down in the living room.

'What's the situation with Danny?' I ask.

'I've left him for good this time. Despite how much he tried to dress it up, he doesn't want anything to do with Niall and that's unforgivable. Do you know anyone who would be interested in a stressed out forty-year-old woman, who looks after a twelve-year-old severely autistic boy?'

'I'm sorry to hear about that.'

'Don't be. You've shown me and Niall more kindness in the last ten days than Danny did in the last ten years.'

'Bringing up Niall on your own has been tough, but you've done an amazing job. Of course his behaviour is unpredictable, but I've seen signs of improvement, even in the past couple of weeks. The pointing to the photos is a massive step forward.'

This is turning into a mutual admiration society.

Almost on cue Niall came into the dining room with an Argos catalogue. He turns to the suitcases page and takes my finger to point at them. I look over at Kerry.

'I think he wants to go on holiday. If you repeat the word of the object he'll be satisfied.'

'Suitcases,' I say, and he immediately flicks onto another page, still holding onto my finger. When we reach the page with the microwave oven, he pushes my finger against the chicken inside the oven.

'Chicken.'

He then moves onto another page. The photo is a toaster and we point to the two slices of toast.

'Toast.'

After a dozen more photos he retreats to the garden, leaving the catalogue behind on the dining room table.

During the course of the next hour Kerry's mood brightens up. She lives an extremely stressful life and the final break up with Danny has added to this, although in the long term it's a good move. I did invite her over tomorrow, but I played down the significance of the concert. The last thing that she needs is me telling her how wonderful it is that Harry is playing the Royal Festival Hall.

I hear Harry come thundering down the stairs, before arriving in the living room.

'Daddy, it's nine-thirteen and I want to go to sleep at nine fifty-six,' he announces.

'You mean that you want to go to *bed* at that time?' I ask.

'No, I want to be *asleep* at nine fifty-six precisely, otherwise I'm going to stay up all night.'

Harry's friend Robert, goes to bed at exactly eighteen minutes past nine every night.

'Well, we can't have that, so let's get moving.'

Harry dashes to the front door.

'Hold on, first of all I want you to say goodbye to Kerry and Niall and then I want to check that you haven't taken any of Niall's DVDs.'

'Cheerio,' Harry mutters quietly, before stretching his arms from his sides in the classic search pose. He knows the routine.

I can't find any of Niall's possessions and seconds later he's standing by my car, waiting for me.

'Niall, come here and say goodbye to David,' Kerry tells her son.

Niall approaches me carrying his Argos catalogue. As far as I'm aware Argos don't sell food, but Niall finds enough electrical appliances that do contain food and we spend the next few minutes pointing.

'Come on, you're wasting my time,' Harry shouts.

'I'll see you tomorrow,' I say to Niall, but he turns around and walks away.

'Sorry about that,' Kerry says, 'he's not into greetings.'

'No problem. Thanks for a lovely meal; it was a nice evening in the end.'

'I should be thanking you for helping me out of my dark mood and for dealing with the situation at the pub.'

We hug tightly before I speed off in the car; the destination being Harry's bedroom.

At nine-thirty-eight I'm lying next to Harry in his bed. It's a balmy night, but as usual my son insists on submerging me with the duvet. When I attempt to give my left foot some air he immediately sits up and pulls the duvet over me again. It's going to be a sweaty night.

It's just after ten when Harry dozes off. It's the earliest he's been to sleep for weeks. The Ipswich trip took its toll. At nine-fifty-eight he glanced at the clock and even though he was very drowsy, he still wanted to get up as it was past his allocated time, however for once his body told him otherwise.

A few minutes later I'm lying on my own bed, thinking about tomorrow. I'm both excited and nervous at the same time. It could be one of the best days ever; or the worst.

In only a few hours, I'll find out.

Royal Festival Hall

I glance at my alarm; it's twenty past four. I notice that the lights are on downstairs and that can only mean one thing.

I find Harry sitting in the kitchen finishing off a cold steak and kidney pie, that was in the fridge, accompanied by a glass of tomato juice. I immediately take them both off him.

'You're going to get sick eating that; the pie is supposed to be cooked.'

'I like it better cold.'

Harry, go to bed and get some sleep.'

'But that's pointless.'

'Get to bed *now*,' I shout at him.

Harry begrudgingly makes his way to his bedroom, while I spend the next fifteen minutes looking for the kitchen door key, to lock it. I hope that Harry gets at least a couple of hours' sleep; otherwise it could be a difficult day.

I flop down on the living room sofa and doze off, but wake up an hour and a half later to hear the words 'Take that, you bastard,' repeated over and over again.

'What are you watching?'

'It's one of your films, Daddy. It's brilliant, there's swearing, killing and lots of women's breasts.'

I must have recorded this film by mistake. I immediately delete it.

'That's not fair. I wanted to see that man's head chopped off again.'

I make a mental note to record a more innocent film. There's a Doris Day and Rock Hudson film on later this morning that should fit the bill. I can't imagine any heads being chopped off in that one.

Although it's only six o'clock, I'm already on edge. I'm beginning to regret inviting everyone over. What was I thinking of?

While Harry is watching TV I tidy up the house. I then set all the snacks on the dining room table. Of course the peanuts and crisps are still in their packets, otherwise there'll be nothing left of them by the time the guests arrive.

'Are you looking forward to the concert?' I ask Harry, as he's getting dressed after his shower.

'It's going to be as boring as the woodwork lessons with Mister Willy.'

'That's Mister Willmore. Are you worried about it?'

Harry stares blankly at me.

'Are you nervous?'

'I don't want to wear polished shoes; they make me feel sick.'

I decide not to pursue this line of questioning.

Laura arrives at eleven o'clock. She's brought along some homemade lasagne, pizza, loads of chicken wings and baked potatoes.

'Wow, you must've been up all night cooking,' I remark as she lays the food down next to my snacks.

'Yeah, I was; but only giving your guests peanuts and crisps is pitiful.'

She's got a point. It's ironic, as I'm always the first one to grumble when we go out to some party, or even a wedding, where the food on display is usually a cold, one-inch sausage on a stick, a miserable piece of pineapple and cheese, again on a stick, and the dismal quarter sandwiches where if you look really hard you might spot a slice of ham or cheese.

'Why are you coming to see me now? You didn't turn up for all the other times when I sang at the school.'

'Edward told us that we couldn't see any of your rehearsals,' Laura explains.

'It's going to be a lump of cow's turd.'

'Harry, please don't talk like that, and I certainly don't want to hear you swearing when you're on stage,' Laura tells him.

'But swearing is the best thing in my life and the people at the concert are going to love it.'

Laura and I look at each other. I sense that she's as nervous as me.

As the guests won't be arriving for a good half an hour, I make coffee for the both of us and we settle down in the kitchen.

'I'm moving in with Sean next week,' Laura reveals.

'That was quick; I thought that you were undecided yesterday.'

'You told me it was the only way of knowing for sure if the relationship is going to work, so I've taken your advice; although by the end of today that decision could be reversed.'

'Depending on Timothy and Mary?'

Laura nods.

'I take it that Sean was pleased?'

'Yes, he was, and I am too, it's just …'

'Harry,' I complete her sentence.

'You've found a good man, Laura, and I hope that it all works out for you,' I say, as I click her coffee mug with mine.

She smiles, but when she looks away from me I notice tears in her eyes. It's an emotional time for her right now. Harry is the key to her future happiness with Sean.

At midday my sister Fiona and her daughter Isabelle arrive.

'I love the idea of a pre-concert party; it's so cool,' Fiona tells me, as we hug.

I look over at Laura , who jokingly rolls her eyes.

'A glass of white?' she asks my sister.

'Oh, go on then.'

'Isabelle, what drink would you like?'

'I don't want anything,' Isabelle responds sullenly.

'It's exciting about Harry playing the Festival Hall tonight, isn't it?' I say.

'Yeah, right.'

I notice a sarcastic tone in her voice.

Harry walks over to Isabelle.

'Did you know that Robert lives at sixteen Tavistock Road in Thornton Heath?' he asks her.

Isabelle's facial expression indicates that she's bored with this conversation already.

'Niall lives at twenty-seven Berry Grove in Streatham and his garden is thirty-two feet long. I know, because I tested it myself.'

'That's amazing.'

'Harry, can you get a bottle of Coke out of the fridge in the kitchen please?'

'But why me?'

'Can you just get it please and don't open it up.'

I approach Isabelle.

'I've observed the way you are with Harry. Because he's not into the latest music or fashions and talks about nerdy things, you completely disregard him. Don't you *ever* talk down to my son again; do you hear me?'

Isabelle nods.

'Because if you do I'll take that iPod of yours and smash it in two, and if you don't think I'll do it, just try me. If you then complain to your mum and dad, I'll apologise to them, but then I'll explain the reason why I did it; how you've treated Harry behind their back. Don't you understand that Harry has a disability?'

She nods again, her face now red with embarrassment.

'I can't force you to be friends with Harry; all I'm asking is that you're civil to him. OK?'

'Yes, Uncle David,' she replies, in a more humble manner.

This may seem an extreme reaction and I didn't expect, or need, a confrontation today, but I'm fed up with the way my niece treats my son.

The next to arrive are Stephanie and Robert.

'It's so lovely of you to invite us, darling. You must be so excited,' Stephanie says, as she kisses me on both cheeks.

'Nervous would be more accurate. And how are you, Robert?'

Robert walks past me and stands in front of the dining room table, intensely studying the food. He grabs a chicken wing, smells it and takes a bite, but immediately spits it out, putting the half-eaten chicken wing back in the dish.

'Fuck me, what's going on here?' he asks.

'What do you mean?'

'What crap did you put on that chicken?'

I pick up another piece and take a bite.

'Garlic, oregano and basil, I think.'

'Have you lost your mind, Mister McCarthy? You've ruined my day.'

Stephanie steps in and clears up the debris.

'I'm sorry about that; he's very fussy about his food.'

I think I picked up on that.

Harry then walks into the room. Harry and Robert don't acknowledge each other, which is the norm.

'Robert, aren't you going to wish Harry good luck for the concert tonight?' Stephanie asks her son.

'I don't like those chicken wings, they smell like pigeon's shit,' Robert tells Harry.

Harry nods.

'Have you got any lemonade, but not a fridge one?' Robert asks me.

'I think I can do that.'

Stephanie follows me into the kitchen.

'So, will there be any single men at this party?' she asks.

'Only me.'

'Oh, OK,' she says, but she cannot hide her disappointment.

Thanks for that morale boaster.

'Perhaps it's for the best. Terry has been wearing me out all week.'

'Terry?'

'You know, the keep fit instructor. His stamina is phenomenal.'

I barely know this woman, but she has no qualms about confiding the most intimate details of her life.

Thankfully the doorbell interrupts our conversation. I open the front door to find Mum standing there with Sean, Timothy and Mary.

'You didn't tell me that Laura was hooking up with this fellow,' Mum says, pointing to Sean.

'I only knew myself a few days ago.'

'She's only been apart from you for five minutes. Does she know what she's doing?'

'Come in, everyone,' I say.

Mum comes in first, followed by Timothy and Mary, who greet me with their customary nods.

'I'm sorry about Mum, she can be a bit full on,' I say to Sean.

'She's a spirited lady, all right.'

We step out to the garden where Mum is already giving Laura a lecture about betraying me, despite the fact that it's been over a year since our divorce. I'm staying clear of that discussion.

Sean acknowledges Laura, but like me, he's keeping a safe distance.

'Did Laura tell you our good news?' Sean asks.

'Yeah, I'm really pleased for both of you.'

The truth is I'm having a hard time dealing with this. After all, a few days ago I didn't know that Sean even existed and now he's about to live with my ex-wife.

Robert walks past us and approaches Timothy.

'And who are you?' Robert asks.

'Timothy.'

'What's your surname?'

'Donovan.'

'Do you know your date of birth?'

Timothy looks at Mary and they both glance at their father.

'June the fourteenth, two thousand and one.'

'Do you like mayonnaise?'

'It's OK,' Timothy replies, with a puzzled expression.

'I prefer butter.'

Timothy nods.

'Do you have a tortoise?'

'No.'

'I love tortoises, because they never get angry. Do you like wallpaper?'

'I'm not sure ...'

'Wallpaper sucks, especially the ones with all those patterns, it makes my eyes go crazy.'

'I see,' Timothy says, but without any hint of sarcasm.

'And what name do you use?' Timothy asks Mary.

'Mary.'

'And what's your surname?'

'Donovan.'

I'm not sure if Robert realises that they are brother and sister.

'What do you think of toilet paper?'

'I don't know.'

'I hate it, especially when my mum cuts my finger-nails and I have to touch the toilet paper after that; it drives me mad.'

Mary smiles at Robert.

'Timothy and Mary seem to be coping better in the autistic world,' I say to Sean.

'They know the consequences if there's *ever* a repeat of the restaurant incident,' he replies.

For the first time I recognise that there could be a future for Laura and Sean. It makes me both happy and sad.

Laura walks into the kitchen and hugs Sean.

'I didn't realise that my role as daughter-in-law is a life long commitment,' she tells Sean and me.

'You can run, but you can't hide,' I say.

'Is Mummy going to live in your house?' Harry asks Sean.

'Yes, she is,' he proudly confirms.

'How many stairs have you got?'

'I don't know.'

'Can you find out?'

'OK.'

'Do you speak properly when you're in your house?'

'Well I ...'

'Sean is from Ireland, so he has an Irish accent; we've told you this before,' Laura interrupts.

Harry looks perplexed.

'Is your house crap?'

'No, it's a nice home.'

'What type of washing machine have you got?'

'It's a Miele.'

'What's the model number?'

'I'm not sure.'

'Can you find out that as well?'

'Yes, as soon as I get home.'

'OK, Harry, that's enough questions for now,' Laura says.

Sean is extremely patient and understanding with Harry, otherwise I'm certain that Laura wouldn't have continued with their relationship.

Ten minutes later Kerry and Niall arrive. Niall, like Robert before him, heads straight to the dining room table. His face is intense as he studies what food is on offer. He looks at the lasagne, and then starts jumping up and down, in anger.

'Calm down and let's get some juice,' Kerry tells him.

I'm standing just behind him and for once I'm antici-pating his next move, as he forcefully pushes away the dish containing the lasagne. I rush to stop him, but I slip and in a second I am lying on my back on the floor, with a dish of lasagne on top of me.

'David, I'm so sorry ...' Kerry utters, before running after Niall, who's heading towards the garden.

Laura is the first to arrive, but instead of helping me, she smiles at my predicament.

'That shirt's a write off; luckily it's only one of your four, ninety-nine, Primark specials,' she adds.

It's Isabelle who hands me a roll of paper towels, and amazingly she hasn't got her customary smug grin.

The lasagne covers my shirt and part of my jeans. Following Laura's advice, I depose of my Primark shirt, throw the jeans in the washing machine, have a quick wash and then return downstairs in new clobber.

'David, what can I say?' Kerry enquires.

'You owe me four pounds and ninety-nine pence.'

'Of course.'

She reaches for her purse.

'Kerry, I'm only joking. It's no big deal, it was my own fault for slipping.'

Niall walks back into the dining room.

'Come over here and say sorry to David,' Kerry tells her son.

'There's no need.'

'Yes, there is. Niall, say sorry.'

For a split second Niall glances at me, before strok-ing my arm with the palm of his hand.

'Are you going to be friends with David?'

He then takes my hand and moves it up and down in an exaggerated handshake. This is the first time that I've seen him do this and I'm moved by it.

'Thank you, Niall.'

His eyes have already diverted to the dining room table and, with the help of Kerry, he picks out the food that he wants and then settles in the garden.

'Presumably he doesn't like lasagne?' I ask Kerry.

'Yes, but that's the first time I've seen him actually throw food away.'

'No harm done, there's plenty more.'

'David, you're so patient with Niall.'

Laura, who is standing nearby, gives me a knowing smile.

'You'll get there in the end with him. I'm no doctor, but judging how Ritalin has helped Harry, I'm sure that it'll control Niall's outbursts.'

'I've resisted giving him any medication up to now, but I've no other option.'

'He looks settled,' I say, as I watch him tuck into his food.

Kerry smiles, but doesn't respond.

Bernadette and Alice are the next to arrive.

'Hello, Mister McCarthy, you're looking a bit thick again today,' Bernadette informs me.

So far, as the host of this party, I've had my sanity questioned, a dish of lasagne dumped on me and been labelled stupid. I must do this again soon.

'Bernadette, apologise right now,' her mother sternly tells her.

'But, Mummy, look at him; I'm not lying.'

'Alice, please don't worry about it.'

'But that was such a dreadful thing to say.'

Bernadette approaches Harry.

'Mummy tells me that you're singing a song in London. Why can't you just do it at the bus stop opposite Streatham Common instead?'

'That's a brilliant idea.'

'No, you're singing at the Royal Festival Hall; it's all been arranged,' I intervene.

'Are the men in the chairs going to be wearing suits?'

'Yes, I suppose some of them will.'

'I don't like men in suits. They're evil bastards.'

'No, they're not, and don't forget , Harry, that you'll be wearing a tie,' I add.

'Make sure that your dad doesn't pull the tie too tight for you, otherwise you'll die and that won't be any good, because I want to go to the new Jim Carrey film with you tomorrow at the Streatham Odeon. It's on at five past twelve, twenty past two and five thirty-five.'

'Cool; I love Jim Carrey, because he's a mad man,' Harry says.

Laura and I smile at each other. A third date; who'd have thought?

'Do you want to chaperone them this time?' I ask Alice.

She nods, while looking at my ex-wife.

'Laura, would you like help me keep an eye on the kids tomorrow?' Alice enquires.

'I'd love to.'

'I want to go to the five minutes past twelve film and that means that we have to leave Bernadette's house at eleven thirty-nine; OK?' Harry asks.

He's looking at me, but Alice and Laura nod. It's in their interest to get to the cinema on time, as the consequences will be twofold; Harry's wrath and two hours of studying the film showing times screen.

Alice helps Bernadette choose her food and as I'm chatting to Laura and Sean I feel my shirt being tugged; it's Bernadette.

'Mister McCarthy, I need some Branston pickle on my pizza,' she says, whilst looking at my chest.

I take the Branston pickle jar out of the fridge and she plops a large teaspoonful on her pizza.

That's a first.

The party continues without any further incidents, and by four o'clock only Laura and Mum are left. I noticed an element of fear in all the guests' eyes as they wished us good luck for tonight. Are they feeling equally apprehensive?

Mum asks me to accompany her, as she approaches Harry.

'Harry, there'll be no playing the fool tonight, OK?' she says.

Harry eventually looks up at her, but doesn't reply.

'Here's three pounds for you.'

'Daddy, how many DVDs can I get for three pounds?'

'One.'

And that's if I add another seven pounds. Mum is on a fixed income, so any amount that she gives is gratefully received, but she still thinks that it's nineteen sixty-five, when for a hundred pounds you could get you a three bedroom detached house, complete with a swimming pool.

Harry looks disappointed at the coins and places them in a spare pair of my shoes, before continuing to watch Bugs Bunny.

'All right, if you're good tonight, I'll give you another three pounds. It's like making a deal with the devil.'

'I've heard of that bloke, I'll like to meet him.'

I expected Mum to say that unless Harry bucks up his ideas, his wish will come true one day, but she doesn't.

'Can you take some photos tonight? But don't bother sending them to me if he beats up the conductor or a member of the audience.'

'I'll bear that in mind.'

'Take care of him, David, OK?'

'Of course.'

Mum looks intensely at me and I see her bottom lip quiver, but she quickly regains her composure.

'Ring me tonight when you get in, with all the news; good or bad.'

'I will.'

We hug, which is rare these days, and then she leaves. It's nice to depart on good terms.

Soon afterwards Harry has another shower and after he's dressed I take a couple of photos of him. He looks so smart in his dark, pressed trousers, white shirt and tie, and of course the polished shoes.

Laura then takes out her digital and takes more photos.

'Enough of these photos; you're wasting my time.'

Harry is always complaining of this, as if he has to dash off for a peace summit at the United Nations. Watching DVDs is just about all he does in his spare time.

One hour later we're greeted at the Royal Festival Hall by an exuberant Edward.

'And how's our star feeling today?' he asks Harry.

'We better be home by five past ten, because Batman is on BBC Three.'

'He's not in the best of moods,' I explain.

'Nerves can take over the most seasoned professional but, Harry, you'll be splendid. I feel that all of your performances so far have led up to the moment you walk on stage today. The audience are going to adore you.'

'I want to go for a crap.'

'That's just nerves,' Edward assures us.

I take him to the toilet and soon after we say our goodbyes to him. Whilst we're feeling tense, he couldn't care less.

We've an hour to kill, so we decide to visit a trendy café on the South Bank.

'Do you think that he'll swear?' Laura asks me, as she takes the first sip of her coffee.

'If I was a betting man, I'd say that it was seventy-thirty in favour of him swearing. He does it everywhere else, so why would he stop just because he's on stage in front of two and a half thousand people, and in a theatre that means nothing to him?'

'Thanks for reassuring me.'

'I'm just giving you an honest answer. I hope I'm wrong. I warned him about taking away his DVDs if he misbehaves, but as you know, that doesn't always work.'

'After the cards that he's been dealt with, he deserves his moment of glory; but it could be a disaster,' Laura says.

I nod, unable to find the correct words.

I desperately want everything to go well for him today. It may not mean a lot to Harry, but it does to his parents.

I even had a word with the man upstairs. I hope he listened.

'I haven't felt this tense since …'

The nervous breakdown are the words that she still cannot say.

The only time that Harry seemed to be affected by Laura's illness was when she didn't feel well enough to cook his dinner. He told her that she was lazy and asked if the McDonalds chef could now live with us.

Although it sounds harsh, Harry's autism caused Laura's breakdown and I lost the only woman that I have ever loved.

'David, what are you thinking about?' Laura asks.

'Just wondering what time we need to leave here.'

Thirty minutes later we're sitting two rows from the front, awaiting Harry's arrival. The twenty-five piece orchestra come out to generous applause, followed by the thirty or so choir, from another school. Harry and five of his school friends are the last group to take their seats. Although they won't be singing for another hour, they still have to remain on stage for the whole show. It's unrealistic to assume that they can keep quiet for such a lengthy period, but it's too late now.

The presenter walks onto the stage to mild applause. He seems vaguely familiar, but I can't think where I've seen him. He's probably been in episodes of *Eastenders* or *Holby City*. He introduces the first musical piece and the orchestra play beautifully for the next fifteen minutes. The choir and orchestra combine for the next half a dozen songs, but my full attention is on Harry. He's surrounded by three teachers, including Edward. After the third song he shouts out, 'hurry up you lot, Batman is on at five past ten.' Luckily the audience laugh; perhaps they think it's part of the act? By the look on the conductor's face, he certainly didn't see the funny side.

The Z list presenter then introduces Harry and his five class friends, taking time to explain that they are special needs pupils. They walk from the back to the middle of the stage, where to my amazement Harry sits behind the piano. All the musicians in the orchestra put down their instruments. Laura and I look at each other with surprise and an element of fear. We both know that he plays the piano, but I didn't think that his skills are sufficient for an event of this magnitude. My blood pressure readings have just gone up a notch or two, I'm sure.

'Hello, my name is Harry and I love Thomas the Tank Engine.'

Mild applause and gentle laughter greet this remark.

'If you've got any spare Thomas DVDs or any telephone directories with you, that you don't want, please leave them on the stage for me.'

A nervous looking Edward wears his customary painted smile, but he's probably seething.

'I'm going to sing and play the piano. I've practised this song fifty-four times now and I'm fed up with it.'

I'm getting increasingly nervous.

'I'll play it again, but this is the last time, OK?'

The audience are now in hysterics and give Harry a warm round of applause. I hope that the singing and piano playing match the build-up.

Edward approaches Harry and has a quiet word in his ear. Edward smiles throughout this exchange.

'I suppose I better get on with it.'

Harry looks at the songbook in front of him and starts to play The Beatles song 'Let It Be'.

I immediately start to cry. His piano playing is superb and his singing is so beautiful. I look over at Laura and she's already reaching for a tissue.

The other special needs children join Harry for the chorus and it all sounds just wonderful. I sit back to fully appreciate what is possibly my proudest moment as a parent.

I'm stunned at his piano playing and the clarity of his voice.

He keeps the standard up for the rest of the song and as soon as he sings his last note Laura and I stand up to applaud, as do most of the audience. Harry walks in front of the piano and starts bowing, he seems genuinely pleased at the audience reaction. The applause lasts for a couple more minutes, until the Z list presenter comes back on stage and warmly shakes Harry's hand. Harry then looks over at us and points to his watch, indicating that it's time to get moving. The pupils then take their seats, but Harry leaves the stage with Edward.

Laura and I instantly make our way to the stage door area.

'I can't believe what I've just seen,' Laura says.

I shake my head; for once I am speechless.

Laura brings me closer to her and we embrace. Inevitably we both start to cry again. It's almost like all the pain and heartache of the past few years have just been exorcised. This may sound over dramatic, but the experience of the past ten minutes almost feels like a miracle.

'Come on, we better go, Harry will be waiting for us,' I say, not before borrowing Laura's tissue to wipe my tears away.

Edward and Harry are awaiting our arrival.

'You were amazing,' Laura tells her son, before hugging him. This time he doesn't resist.

'Yeah, that wasn't half bad,' Harry agrees.

'We're both very proud of you, Harry, and next week I'm going to get you a piano so that you can practice more,' I say.

'Can I have a yellow one?'

'That might be a bit difficult, but we'll see.'

Harry seems receptive to the idea, which is another giant step forward.

'Your piano playing was just like Liberace and Paul McCartney himself couldn't have sung it any better,' Edward announces.

Steady on, old chap, let's not get too carried away here.

'This is my most fulfilling moment as a music teacher. Harry and the class were magnificent.'

'Where are the rest of the class?'

'We're supposed to be on stage until the end, but I thought it's best to take Harry out.'

'Thank you; that's appreciated.'

'Harry, I told you the audience would adore you. Now you better get going before those autograph hunters track you down. I've got to sneak back on stage, I'll see you on Monday.'

'Don't forget to buy me that Thomas DVD you promised me.'

'I'll have one for you on Monday.'

'I want *Thomas and Friends – Calling All Engines*.'

'You've got it,' Edward confirms before dashing off.

The mystery of what Edward whispered in his ear has been revealed.

'Can I play here again next Saturday?' Harry asks.

'No, but we'll ask at the school about other concerts.'

Harry isn't quite up to the superstar status where he'll have a long-term residency gig like Elton John does in Las Vegas, but given time …

Our expectations for Harry were simple. No swearing and avoid embarrassing himself. I couldn't envisage that he would be a success. My thoughts were just focused on damage limitation.

'I'm so glad you enjoyed it,' Laura tells Harry.

'Those other idiots were on for forty-nine minutes and seven seconds. They were too slow and full of shit. Why didn't that crowd boo them?'

'You didn't like them, but the audience did,' Laura explains.

'I have to do lots of concerts now, as I want more DVDs and pianos.'

If giving Harry a DVD is an incentive for every musical performance, then I'll happily oblige, but I'll have to re-negotiate his contract regarding the extra pianos.

We're all still in an elated mood by the time we arrive back at the house. I pour myself and Laura a glass of red wine while Harry rushes upstairs.

'He seems excited,' Laura says.

'Yes, it'll be lovely if this will trigger a musical interest for him.'

Almost on cue Harry starts singing 'Let It Be' from his bedroom.

'That must be the fifty-sixth time that he's sung that song and quite frankly I'm getting fed up of hearing it,' Laura jokingly remarks.

We both laugh and take another sip of wine.

The last time that I felt this euphoric was when Harry was born. It has been an extremely stressful twelve years since that beautiful day and Laura has been with me every step along the way; even after the divorce. It's appropriate that I'm sharing this special day with her.

'Everything seemed to go well with Timothy and Mary,' I say.

'Yeah, I'm still apprehensive about Harry staying at Sean's, but today has given me hope.'

I smile and nod. The fact that Laura seems happy for the first time in years has helped ease my anxiety over her moving in with Sean.

'Now all I want is for you to find someone,' she adds.

'One day maybe, but I'm OK for now.'

Laura nods her response.

'I rang Bryan and Phil earlier, they want to meet up,' I say

Bryan and Phil are my old university friends.

'It's been ages since you've seen them.'

'Yeah, a few years. I've also got someone from Social Services coming over next week to discuss overnight respite. I've decided it's about time I had a social life.'

'That's great news. Let me know when you want me to look after Harry.'

'Thanks, I will.'

'What about your job? Are you still worried about that?' Laura asks.

'Yes I am, but despite the fact that Clarence is a complete arsehole, for some reason I now feel confident that he'll get me a job. He's very driven, and that can only help me. Another glass?' I ask, holding the wine bottle.

'No, thanks, I'm exhausted and want to get back home.'

I help clean up Laura's dishes and load them into her car.

'Thanks again for the food,' I tell her as she opens the driver's seat door.

'No problem, but the next time try using a knife and fork when eating the lasagne.'

We laugh together. The last couple of days have been the most serene period in our relationship for such a long time. I suppose I have Sean to thank for that.

'It's been a wonderful day, I shall never forget it,' she says.

We hug, before she gets into her car.

'Remember to ring your mum,' she adds.

'Thanks for spoiling the moment,' I joke, as I wave her goodbye.

It's nearly one o'clock in the morning before I lie down with Harry.

I start thinking about the past twelve days. In that period I've been attacked several times by Niall, witnessed his epileptic fit and was partly responsible for nearly killing him. I also lost Harry and Robert in the wilds of Streatham, was diagnosed with high blood pressure and thrown out of a West End theatre. I then discovered that Laura has a boyfriend and is now moving in with him. In addition to this, I was made redundant, failed my first interview in spectacular fashion and nearly got arrested for speeding. Laura and I finally put our differences to one side and visited a residential school in Ipswich, which had its stressful moments, but it was ultimately a rewarding day, on many levels.

It would have been nice if my time with Harry had been more peaceful, but that is rare in the autistic world.

I've also grown closer to Kerry and Niall, and have been humbled to see, first hand, how difficult life is for a severely autistic child. I hope to see much more of them in the future.

Harry and Bernadette's relationship may be unconventional, but it's a joy to witness. I am delighted that Laura is going along to the cinema with Alice tomorrow, to be part of their date.

Words cannot describe how proud I am of Harry tonight after his musical performance. It's lovely to see something positive occurring in his life.

I've loved spending some quality time with Harry and I'll miss him terribly when I return to work on Monday.

'Did you enjoy *the Dark Knight Rises* DVD?' I ask my bed companion.

'Not bad, but Adam West should be Batman, because the nineteen sixty-six film was one hundred and five minutes, but *The Dark Knight Rises* is one hundred and sixty-five minutes, so Adam West catches the villains quicker than Christian Bale.'

I can't argue with that logic.

'What was the film about?'

'Fighting.'

'What else?'

'Jumping on roofs.'

I think we've covered the plot.

'Are you excited about getting a piano?'

'Yeah, can we put it in the bathroom? I want to play the piano after I've done a …'

'No, we'll put it in the living room,' I interrupt.

We do have a good-size bathroom, but it's not big enough for a piano. It would be a good conversation piece though.

'Are you looking forward to going to Sean's house tomorrow?'

'I want to eat Sean's garden ants, to see if they are better than ours.'

Welcome to autism, Sean.

'What do you want to do after visiting Sean's house?'

'I want to go back to your house.'

'That's nice.'

'Because the bricks in your house are the best that I've ever seen.'

It's always nice to get a compliment, even a brick one.

'OK, Harry, it's time to go to sleep.'

I lean over and kiss his forehead. Harry's only reaction is to check that all the bed clothes are covering me.

I doze off, but wake up a few hours later to find Harry sitting up on his bed, singing the Robbie Williams' song 'Angels'.

Even in my sleepy demeanour I notice a subtle change in the lyrics. The female angel offers love and affection, and promises that she won't forsake the person she wants to protect.

Harry replaces the word *she* with *he*.

I'm almost certain that he's not aware of the full meaning behind his lyric change, but just for tonight I can pretend that was his intention.